P9-CRE-413

You are a woman of WISDOM, courage, strength, compassion & creativity...

Go forth with the FIRE of CONFIDENCE in your heart, kindle it with care, & never let its brilliant flame go out!

Caroline Joy Adams

A Woman of Wisdom

Words have tremendous power...

and words of inspiration can contribute to our healing...
They can change our very perceptions of ourselves,
our attitudes, our entire way of thinking about who we are,
and what our place in the world might be...

A Woman of Wisdom

Honoring & Celebrating Who You Are

Caroline Joy Adams

CELESTIAL ARTS
Berkeley, California

Celestial Arts
P.O. Box 7123
Berkeley, California 94707

Distributed in Canada by Ten Speed Canada, in the United Kingdom and Europe by Airlift Books, in New Zealand by Southern Publishers Group, in Australia by Simon & Schuster Australia, in South Africa by Real Books, and in Singapore, Malaysia, Hong Kong, and Thailand by Berkeley Books.

Cover and interior design by Caroline Joy Adams
Interior illustrations by Caroline Joy Adams

Library of Congress Cataloging-in-Publication Data
on file with the publisher

A HEART AND STAR BOOK

First printing, 1999
Printed in Singapore

1 2 3 4 5 6 7—03 02 01 00 99

Dedicated to my greatest inspiration of all,
my dearest daughter, Kristen,
with infinite love
& great joy

CONTENTS

PART I

Honoring Your Journey, Past and Present
Looking into the Seven Mirrors of Self-Reflection

PART II

Moving Forward Upon Your Life Path
The Seven Pathways to Celebrating Who You Are

May the resounding chorus of wondrous words that sings forth from these pages soothe your spirit, stimulate your mind, seep into your soul...and may they encourage you to awaken to your deepest self.

Within these pages lives a series of questions for you to ask yourself—eye-opening, soul-stretching, potentially life-changing ones. For living in—and changing with—the questions is the very core of our journey. And by forever opening ourselves to new answers, we can best proceed along the pathway, wherever the quest leads us.

Use the questions and inspirations within in whatever way most calls out to you. Take however much time you need or want, and let them speak to you when the time is right. Just follow your intuition, now and always. As you travel through the rich and varied landscape of these pages, and of your life, may you enjoy the journey ahead!

the Invitation

The Vision

This book came into being because of a great dream of my own—a vision that resides within my heart that we women, everywhere, may someday come to *feel*, deep within ourselves, a much greater sense of our own beauty, wisdom, and strength. We are all traveling the pathway of becoming our most courageous, noble, and loving selves—and it is time that we come to *know* ourselves as the gifted, creative beings that we are.

As an artist and writer on a spiritual quest, I have long been aware of the great power of words and images to illuminate our life paths, for I have been deeply touched, changed, and influenced by the writing of so many others along my own journey. As a child, I spent almost all my time dreaming and drawing, reading and writing, and was constantly buried in books. My favorite ones featured marvelous characters, magical themes, and magnificent endings. Books such as the classic tale *The Secret Garden* helped me believe that each of our lives is a story, and no matter how difficult things seem in the present, the future can always unfold in new ways.

As I grew and matured, my quest to understand the compelling individual life stories that make up the fabric of humanity eventually led me to a degree in counseling psychology. The mysterious and magnificent story of the universe—of all life—has also held never-ending fascination for me. This has impelled me to explore the gardens of the spirit, through the writings and teachings of many great women and men who have inspired my own search for truth.

As a result, some time ago my own writing turned toward messages of the heart and spirit, and I created a series of colorfully designed posters and prints, inscribed with words I had written, which I called *Inspirations*. My intention through these offerings is to encourage us to see the stories of our lives as the ever-challenging, yet always *sacred journeys* that they are—that we may experience as great an appreciation for ourselves as possible, each step of the way.

For we all, at the deepest level of our souls, at the fundamental core of our beings, are in great need of recognition and appreciation of who we are. We need it from the moment we enter this world until the moment we leave this earth—we truly cannot exist for long, much less thrive, without it. We need to receive it from others, to give it to others, and at the same time, we need to develop the capacity to give it to ourselves.

Our most joyful moments in life usually occur when we have a sense of being truly seen, felt, and heard, when we are feeling loved and acknowledged for who we really are. Our most intense psychic pain, on the other hand, comes from *not* receiving the recognition that we crave. For we all want to know that others see us as special, beautiful, worthy, and lovable, and yet at the very same time, we *can* come to experience a greater sense of love and appreciation for ourselves.

My hope is that this book will become your guide through this important, highly personal, ongoing process. I created it in response to requests I received from people all over the country to expand some of my most popular *Inspirations* writings into the form of a book. It has been quite a journey, from the initial vision into the reality that you now hold in your hands—with many moments of both challenge and great joy, all along the way.

I offer this to you now as a gift book, in the fullest sense of the word—for whether you have given it to yourself, or have received it from someone else, it is here to encourage you to fully and finally honor the great gift of yourself!

You Are Invited...

This is a personal invitation to you to participate in a unique and exhilarating process, of self-discovery and celebration. An inner voyage, it will give you a pathway to greater acknowledgment and appreciation of who you are. For although you may not live in daily awareness of this truth...you are already a woman of wisdom, depth, and radiant inner beauty; of grace, dignity, and spirit; of clear insight and infinite light. You are rich with the vastness of your life experience, and you have a myriad of special and wondrous gifts to share.

For no matter your age or life stage, your background or beliefs...wherever you are, on your unique yet universal life journey...you are a woman on a quest to live a life of meaning and purpose, of ever-increasing love, and of closest connection to yourself and those around you...

And you are ever-evolving, growing and changing, transforming and recreating yourself, as you travel the luminous and never-ending pathway of self-discovery that is the essence of this quest...

You are continually embracing challenges, acting with courage, looking deeply into the darkness, and making your way back to the light...and accessing your greatest strengths in the process...

You are opening to new possibilities, overcoming your fears, taking risks, creating new and magical dreams and visions for your life when former ones fall away...and you are then planting the seeds and taking the actions to bring them to fruition...

You are listening more often to your inner voice, your ever-present intuition, which encourages you to follow your heart's song, seek your own truths, and speak them aloud...

You are searching for and finding your unique gifts...and you are finding your source of power from within, using it wisely and well...and at the same time pursuing your passions, and finding your true purpose in this world...

And you are learning, at last, the vast importance of nurturing yourself. You are beginning to treat yourself with the kindness and care that you most surely deserve! You are coming to realize that your presence makes a profound difference in the lives of those around you, and in order to fully love others, it is essential to love yourself also...

It is now time for you to acknowledge this great quest that you are on—and to honor and celebrate who you are becoming. May this book be an affirmative and empowering companion as you do so.

May it also inspire you to continue growing and expanding—that you may consciously create a life full of the richest possible expression of yourself—one that is an extraordinary, unfolding testament to your greatest visions and deepest dreams!

You are about to embark
on a majestic inner voyage,
a journey of
self-discovery,
an exciting awakening
to the magnificent essence
of who you are...

Caroline Joy Adams

The Journey Ahead

A Woman of Wisdom is essentially a journey in two parts. Part One, "The Seven Mirrors of Self-Reflection," is about honoring the past and the present by looking deeply within, to gain a heightened awareness of the importance of all that has led you to where and who you now are. Part Two, "The Seven Pathways to Celebrating Who You Are," explores ways of creating more moments of calm, contentment, and joy in your daily life. The Seven Pathways also encourage you to move more confidently forward, to become even more committed to the marvelous visions for the future that you are now creating and bringing into being.

Within each mirror and pathway, you will find some key questions to consider. You may answer some or all of them as you go along, at a later time, or not at all. Whatever feels right to you will be fine. It may be that your journey will be a richer, fuller experience if you do choose to contemplate some of them and write down your answers, for the very act of writing can be a powerful tool of inner transformation—which can lead to very real outward changes at the same time.

If you choose to answer the questions in writing, here is what you will need:

1. A Special Notebook. Use any blank or lined journal or notebook that you like. Try to find one that feels very personal and comfortable. If you prefer writing on your computer, that is fine, too.

2. Pens, pencils, colored markers. Try to write with something that you really enjoy using, something that feels good in your hand and lets your inner voice flow forth without hesitation or frustration. You may want to take a trip to an art or stationery store to buy a few new pens just for this purpose. You may wish to keep the pens in a special place, along with your journal, so they will await you whenever inspiration comes.

3. Time. Yes, this is the one thing we *never* have enough of! Just remember that learning to more fully honor who you are is an incredibly important use of your time, and do try to make a special time to devote to it on a regular basis. A few hours at a stretch once a week would be wonderful, but even brief periods here and there will be of great value.

4. A special atmosphere. You may find your experience will be enhanced if you can at times create a special atmosphere as you begin your reading and writing sessions. You might light a candle to help create a contemplative mood, or put on some of your favorite, most relaxing music. You may wish to center yourself first through a few moments of silent meditation or prayer. Whatever you can do to create a special space in which to spend this precious inner voyaging time will contribute to its empowering effect!

You may also want to share this journey with others. Perhaps after you have gone through the book first on your own, you may want to form a small group of women to explore some of the topics together. Even if you start off with just one or two friends in an informal way, you can offer each other support and encouragement along the way. You may find this can add a wonderful dimension to the experience.

My fondest hope is that my words,
and those of the other women whose words
have been woven into the texture of these pages,
will be a catalyst for you to begin to find your own voice,
and to bring it forth most fully...

As it does come forth, it will be strengthened
in the process. You will discover more about who you are
from that voice...and about where you need
and want to be on your life journey...

And in time, may your inner voice
become most visibly aligned with your outer voice...
May you discover, finally, that
your voice is none other than the sound of your soul,
whispering its deepest truths to you in each moment,
committing pen to paper, speaking aloud
with openness, with clarity and courage,
ever richer, more vibrant, and alive...

Now may the journey begin, and
may it be for you a wonderful and enlightening
adventure of the spirit!

Part One.

Looking into the Seven Mirrors of Self-Reflection

Become aware
of how far
you have already
come...

Realize that you have already
accomplished much more
than you have imagined...

Caroline Joy Adams

Honoring Your Journey

Looking into the Seven Mirrors of Self-Reflection

In the first part of our journey, you will be looking into seven different mirrors. Think of each one as a *beautiful reflecting pool, of still, clear, luminous water—inviting you to look deeply within*. Each mirror is connected and related to the next, and will reflect back to you the deepest parts of your radiant, beautiful self, illuminating your life story in a richer, fuller way than ever before. As you move along from one mirror to another, my hope is that you will be able to see yourself more clearly, and to open to deeper levels of self-awareness, understanding, and appreciation.

Each of these seven mirrors asks you to consider a slightly different aspect of your life. These include the many changes and challenges that you have handled over time with grace, strength, and wisdom, and the myriad ways that you are *now* acting with courage and creativity and taking steps toward your deepest dreams.

You may feel that you have much farther still to travel in all of these regards. At the same time, it is important to become aware of how far you have already come. When you take the time to recognize the ways in which you have made significant progress, you will almost surely realize that you have evolved more fully, accomplished much more, and come much farther than you have imagined.

1.

The Mirror of Change

Honoring

Your Continual Process of Growth & Change

We are forever
changing, growing,
evolving, emerging
into more of whom we are meant to be...
& Growth awaits us always,
indeed infinitely invites
us in ...

Caroline Joy Adams

You Are a Woman Forever Changing, Growing, Emerging, and Evolving...

I invite you first to take a few moments, look into a real mirror, and imagine it to be the *Mirror of Change*. Look deeply into your own eyes, and contemplate this question: *What are the three most compelling and important changes you would make in your life right now if you could?*

By looking clearly into those radiant, glowing mirrors of your soul, you will see your deepest wishes rising to the surface, making it easy for you to name these three changes. Essentially, you are always in the process of asking yourself these all-important questions: *What changes do you most desire to come about? What are the changes that you require to come about, if you are to be true to who you are, and to ultimately experience a measure of satisfaction in all of the important arenas of your life: relationships, family, work, and more?*

What a delicately woven and complex fabric of changes each of our lives really is! For the endless process of change is a fundamental, essential part of the quest we are all on to discover our true selves. Indeed, as we journey through life, the endless cycles of change that we move through continually shape, mold, and change us into who we now are.

At times we have clear choices about the changes that are possible, and can purposefully and consciously bring them about. But at other times, we are required to weather changes brought about by the choices and actions of others—or by outward circumstances far beyond the realm of our control. These changes may be thrust upon us, completely against our will, every fiber of our being screaming out in resistance—yet to no avail. Our only choice then may be to shift our *perspective*.

This is when I find it helpful to call forth my deep-rooted belief that everything—and *everyone*—can become our teachers, if we continually open to the lessons that are being offered. Powerful and constant, welcome or not, these lessons are forever presenting themselves to us. What if each lesson is here to deepen our awareness and understanding of ourselves and others, and to allow us to access ever-deeper layers of the inner core of courage, strength, insight, wisdom, and love that is the essence of who we are?

I believe that it is a continual, empowering, and moment-to-moment choice to see life from this understanding. This strong sense that there is a reason for all that occurs in our lives is what enables me to keep going in the face of great difficulty, and it is what I consider to be the heart of true wisdom. Wisdom is also about living in the full awareness that our individual life stories are none other than works-in-progress of the most marvelous kind. As such, we are forever changing, growing, evolving, emerging into more of whom we are meant to be.

Change also asks us to grow—in every direction possible—to grow, eternally, into an expanded version of our former selves. And as we grow and change, we return to the same fundamental questions, over and over again: *What changes do we feel that we most need to make, what do we most want to happen in our lives, and whom do we most want to become?*

At the same time as we ask the questions anew, it is also important to take the time to honor and to reflect upon our past experiences. By developing as great an awareness as possible of where we have been, we can move forward with a clearer vision of where we are headed.

When I take the time to contemplate the many changes that I have gone through in my own life, and am experiencing even at present, I often have to remind myself of this fact: life itself really *is* growth and change. The moment we stop growing and changing, we are no longer alive. And the most significant changes are the greatest learning opportunities of all.

But there are times when I wish I could stop the raging river of change from flowing in my life. If only I could just float for a while in a place of peace and tranquillity, of quietude and calm, where the floodgates of change would be closed, and no major changes would be *allowed* to occur!

Yet I also know that it is my most major life change—the experience of becoming a mother—that has brought about my greatest growth. Before Kristen, my now nine-year-old daughter, was born, I had no idea of the immensity of the task that lay before me, or how completely she would change my life in every way. Her presence calls forth everything there is within me—from the most intense, fiercely protective love to the deepest fears and frustrations. My most potent emotions have all been heightened to new levels by having her by my side so much of the time, and in my heart every waking moment.

She has caused me to grow in so many ways I can only begin to describe them, and the process only intensified when she became mine to raise entirely on my own. At the time, such a traumatic life change felt like one of the most devastating kind. It came to me not by my own choice, but by the choice of another—yet altered my life in every conceivable way. It also accelerated even further the deep process of growth in which I was already immersed—as I am sure that your most significant life changes have done for you.

My hope is that you can now begin to see your life story as the magnificently unfolding tale of a woman who has lived through many changes, and gained great wisdom in the process—who has brought great love and beauty into the world, while in a continuous process of learning and growing—and deserves to be honored for all she has been through.

So take some time now to look into the *Mirror of Change* that reflects the river of change and growth flowing through your own life. Here are the questions it asks:

What are the most profound changes that have occurred in your life? How did you feel about them at the time? Did you initiate them, did they come upon you against your desire, or was it some combination of both?

What are the most powerful lessons that you learned from these major changes? How have these lessons changed who you are and the very direction of your life?

In what ways has each change facilitated your growth?

What are the most important ways in which you are growing and changing at present? How do you feel about these changes right now?

What are the three most significant changes that you would like to bring about in the near or distant future? How would you feel if these changes were to take place?

2.

The Mirror of Challenge

Acknowledging

Your Greatest Challenges & Strengths

Challenge

is a DRAGON
with a gift in its mouth ...
Tame the dragon
& the gift is yours ...

— Noela Evans

You Are a Woman Who Faces Challenges
with Strength, Gaining Courage
and Wisdom in the Process...

Change and challenge are closely related, and often follow one another, although they are not always intertwined. Just as life is a constant cycle of changes, it is also a continuous series of challenges: small ones, large ones, every day, every year, at every stage along the way. It starts in infancy, when we must begin to face the challenges of learning to communicate our needs: to crawl, walk, run, speak, make sense of the world around us, deal with our own raw and powerful emotions, and navigate the emotional complexities of family life.

Those innumerable life challenges only increase as we grow and mature. As adults, they include: healing from childhood wounds, finding and maintaining healthy relationships, perhaps becoming parents ourselves, finding satisfactory work, and dealing with a vast array of other emotionally charged issues and circumstances of everyday life. While some people confront overwhelming challenges at every turn, others have relatively smooth pathways through life. The rest of us, it seems, are somewhere in between.

You have certainly known challenges of your own. And you have been forced to face them, even when you didn't want to, even when you wished more than anything on earth that you could magically make them disappear—and prevent them from ever returning. Sometimes the challenges have resolved themselves with time. Other times you have had to go through heroic efforts to get through them and in the process have altered the course of your entire life.

*For you are forever being asked
to confront great changes, and deep challenges...
and to embrace them, one at a time, or sometimes
seemingly all at once...with all the strength and dignity
and courage that you can summon up from deep within,
moment by moment by moment...and by so doing,
you are shaping your life story
into one of power repossessed, wisdom accessed,
healing brought forth, authenticity restored,
dreams and destiny discovered...
and danced into existence...*

While on the pathway to discovering our destiny, so often we seem to be required to dance with the "dragons" of challenge. As Noela Evans says in *Meditations for the Passages and Celebrations of Life*, "Challenge is a dragon with a gift in its mouth. Tame the dragon and the gift is yours."

At times, especially when we are immersed in our most difficult challenges, it is very hard to look beyond the deep and real pain of the moment. Yet if we can make the shift in perspective that allows us a glimpse of the larger, long-term picture—we just may be able to see the deep learning, potential blessings, and gifts that may indeed later arise.

The gifts *will* come in time, and when they do, they will be just as real as the challenges that precipitate them, and a stronger sense of self is almost surely going to be among them, whatever the nature of the challenge. As Clarissa Pinkola Estes says in *Women Who Run With the Wolves*, "Strength does not come after one climbs the ladder or the mountain, nor after one makes it—whatever that 'it' represents. Strengthening oneself is essential to the process of striving, especially before and during—as well as after."

As we traverse the rough terrain of challenging life situations, we rarely feel we possess the strength we would wish for. Yet all the while we are *becoming* stronger, though we don't always perceive this truth in the moment.

Your greatest personal challenges may not be behind you—but perhaps you are facing them right now. At many times in my life, I would have said without hesitation on any given day that this was true for me, as I have moved through a great many challenging life phases. As a child, I lived in a home rife with the continual emotional chaos caused by my parents' very unhappy marriage, until they finally divorced when I was nineteen. And although I had somehow imagined that life would become easier once I left home, that fantasy was quickly dispelled. Instead, my time as a college student, and the following years of my early twenties, were full of new and great challenges.

These included trying to determine what my life work was, beginning to heal from some of my childhood experiences, and learning to live on my own. I was also constantly searching for the deep understanding and intimacy with another person that I had always craved. As a result, I ended up going through a series of agonizing love relationships—ones that always seemed to end for me in great pain, trauma, and disappointment.

Then came my marriage, at age twenty-seven, to a man who had within him both an enormously sweet, generous, loving side and a great well of anger, which created a constant daily interplay of moments of love and forgiveness, deep confusion and fear. Several years later, when my daughter was three, I also lost a second, much wanted child through an emotionally draining and physically excruciating miscarriage. Two years after that, the loss of my marriage brought me to this last five-year-long life phase, of traveling the often fiercely lonely and stressful landscape of life as a single parent.

Strength

does not come AFTER
one climbs the ladder or the mountain
nor after one "makes it" — whatever
that "it" represents.

Strengthening oneself is
essential to the PROCESS
of striving — especially
before & during — as
well as AFTER!

Clarissa Pinkola Estés

Yet I now know that my greatest challenges—especially those that have been most harrowing at the time—have also allowed me to bring forth my greatest capabilities from deep within. And I am sure that those challenges that have touched you at the deepest level of your own heart, mind, and soul have also brought forth your greatest capacities and strengths.

What I often find helpful, when living through a phase of strong challenges, is to take some time to think about what life really looked like at specific points in the past. Sometimes this can give us a new perspective about the present, as we come to realize that we *did* manage to move through challenges that seemed overwhelming and nearly insurmountable at the time. This can remind us that we do have within us the strength and inner resources to meet even the greatest of challenges, once more, whenever called for.

So take some time now and look into your own *Mirror of Challenge*. Consider the dragons you have tamed, or are taming now—and the gifts that have resulted, or are coming into fruition within you now. Also think about the specific strengths you have acquired as a result of wrestling with these challenges and finding your way through to the other side.

What are the most significant challenges you have faced in the past? How did it feel to confront and work through them?

How many of these specific challenges still exist in precisely the same form as they did then? How have they shifted? How did you resolve some of them over time?

What strengths have you developed as a result of facing these particular challenges? What gifts have your challenges allowed you to realize within yourself that would have otherwise remained undiscovered?

What are your most pressing current challenges? What strengths do you feel you are now developing as you respond to them?

3.

The Mirror of Transformation

Overcoming

Your Fears

on the Pathway to Your Dreams

This is
the moment
of transformation
for all of us... None of us
relishes facing our fear, but our
dream exists beyond the border
of that fear...

Mary Manin Morrissey

*You Are a Woman Overcoming Your Fears
on the Way to Your Dreams
and Embracing New Possibilities All Along the Way...*

As Mary Manin Morrissey states in *Building Your Field of Dreams,* "This is the moment of transformation for all of us. None of us relishes facing our fear, but our dream exists beyond the borders of that fear." Yet what often stops us from even beginning to access our true gifts and enter the realm of our dreams is fear. At times, it is so tremendously difficult to get beyond that underlying fear and to force ourselves to move forward. But we just cannot let ourselves be confined by those deep-rooted fears to a life of limitation, of unlived dreams.

*For everything worth really doing or having
requires that we move forward in new directions,
take courageous risks, release and let go of our fears...
that we open our hearts fully...enter the space
of openness to new possibilities...
and allow our courage to come forth
and override our fear...*

Sometimes our fears are so strong because we intuitively sense that we are about to be asked to step through a powerful doorway of transformation, into a new realm that we are afraid we are not prepared to enter. It may be one we would not freely choose to enter, one we would never consciously invite ourselves into. Yet we find ourselves forcibly swept inside anyway, and *are simply not allowed to exit* until we have learned the deep lessons the place within is offering us.

This experience takes us to the very core of our selves. I know that walking through the doorway of my own fears and out the other side has been one of the most powerfully transformative experiences of my life. For seven long and difficult years, I was married to a man whom I loved deeply, but whose unhealed childhood wounds spilled over into all aspects of our relationship, making even the most basic communication often impossible. Still, I was intensely committed to doing everything in my power to make the marriage work, thinking that it would be best for my daughter to keep our family together.

But a part of me, underneath it all, stayed in the marriage not only because of the love that was present and quite real, but also from a deep sense of fear. I was terrified of the very idea of having to survive on my own as the sole support of my daughter and myself, should he ever leave us. Yet one unforgettable May morning—ironically, it was Mother's Day, the year that my daughter was just five—he made his choice.

No longer able to deal with his own emotional demons and remain a husband and father, he packed his possessions and drove off at sunrise in a rental truck, leaving me to pick up the pieces of my life alone. Overnight I was transformed into a single mother of a young child, unaware of my real resources, and suddenly forced to confront the deepest fear of my life. I was overwhelmed at first, almost paralyzed, afraid I would never be able to cope with this new life circumstance.

Gradually, over the first year or two, I moved, one slow step at a time, through all the stages of grieving and layers of fear. I began to peel them away, one by one by one, replacing them with layers of new awareness and newfound strength and confidence—awareness that yes, I *could* go on alone and learn to take care of myself. I could handle being a single parent to my child. I could make a home for us, one that was modest perhaps, but infinitely and finally peaceful—and increasingly full of joyful moments, gratitude, and love.

All things of
Beauty
are birthed from the
Darkness
into the Light...

Caroline Joy Adams

When a woman
rises up in glory

her energy is magnetic
& her sense of

possibility

contagious!

Marianne Williamson

It has been a long, hard journey, and an empowering and exhilarating one as well. Along the way, I have come to let go of many of my preconceived ideas of how life should be lived, or can be lived. In reality, since change is constant, we simply must be able to navigate the journey wherever it takes us—with all the grace and wisdom that we can possibly call forth at every stage.

As a result of this unexpected turn in my own life journey, I now have an inner knowing that I can walk through the fire of my deepest fears—and I can survive, and even thrive once again. This has brought me to a place of openness to all possibilities—which feels like a fine place to be. For the journey of life really is a mysterious and magnificent adventure, and a new chapter of our lives, one brimming with infinite possibilities, is before us at every moment, just waiting to unfold.

As Marianne Williamson says in *A Woman's Worth*, "When a woman rises up in glory, her energy is magnetic, and her sense of possibility contagious!" But in order to get to the place where we can shine forth, radiant with possibility, we often do have to traverse first through the darkest of times. I imagine that you too have at times had to face the darkness and find your way back towards the light—and have been transformed in powerful ways in the process. *For all things of beauty truly are birthed from the darkness into the light...*

Live now for a few moments with these questions. As you look deeply into the *Mirror of Transformation*, take some time to acknowledge yourself for every deep fear you have had to confront and overcome and every new possibility that you have opened to or are opening to right now!

What new possibilities are you now creating or opening up to in your life?

What are the fears you have had to confront and overcome along the way?

How has it felt to have moved through some of those fears?

In what ways are you now transforming yourself and rising up and becoming more of who you are meant to be? What fears are you working through right now in the process?

4.

The Mirror of Truth & Intuition

Listening

to Your Inner Voice

Seek

your **Truth**

& Speak your truth

For there is power in your visions
& in your words ...

Caroline Joy Adams

You Are a Woman Seeking Your Own Truths, Finding and Honoring Your Many Selves, and Beginning to Listen to Your Intuition...

"Our deepest wishes are whispers of our authentic selves. We must learn to respect them. We must learn to listen," Sarah Ban Breathnach gently reminds us in *Simple Abundance.*

An important turning point in my own journey of learning to listen more attentively to my inner voice took place six years ago, when I was participating in a women's spirituality group at a church I was then attending. One of our most memorable group meetings occurred one fine evening when a long, cold winter was nearly at its end, and the wind moved lightly through the night, carrying with it the magical scents of a very welcome spring. That night we created together a beautiful and sacred space, with candles of all sizes and colors arranged in a circle, illuminating the darkness, and fresh flowers as a centerpiece, lighting our hearts with the promise of the gorgeous gardens that we would soon be planting.

We gathered that evening to experience a guided visualization, which asked us to take a special journey that would lead us to find our *place of power within.* Once we had reached this interior place, we were asked to find some words or symbols that we could remember to take back with us into our daily lives, as a reminder of how it felt to be in that space of empowerment. This visualization was a profound experience for me. The message that came to me was that I am most able to feel a sense of my own power when I am in a moment of deep connection with another person— and also when accessing my greatest creativity and sharing it with others. Here are the words that came to me that night: *Seek your truth, and speak your truth, for there is power in your visions and in your words...*

The next day I wrote those words out on a small peach-colored piece of paper with a dark blue calligraphy marker. I positioned it on my refrigerator at eye level, where it would be easily seen. Every time I passed through my kitchen and noticed its message beckoning, I was called to remembrance of the importance of seeking, speaking, and living my truth.

Soon afterwards, I began thinking about how wonderful it would be to have a great variety of empowering phrases set in different places all over my home. I was then overcome with a burst of creative energy. Words and images seemed to present themselves to me, calling out to be put into tangible form. They came to me by night in my dreams, and flowed through me freely throughout the days.

The call was too strong to ignore, and I began to listen. These words made their way onto paper, and within weeks, I had dozens of inspiring messages written out, surrounded by colorful border designs. Showing them to friends, I received rave reactions and encouragement to make them available to others. Before long, I decided to do just that, and found myself deeply immersed in producing the first series of magnets and small framed prints that I called *Inspirations*. Still completely unaware of the immense complexity of the business I was now creating, I soon began selling them in stores nationwide.

One ironic aspect of how this work of mine evolved is that even though I have a gift for the calligraphic art form, several years earlier I had completely given this up, and had actually given away every last calligraphy pen, can of paint, brush, marker, and art supply that I had accumulated over the previous fifteen years! In retrospect, this seems rather short-sighted. Why would I have done such a thing? For I had spent most of my life believing that being an artist was my main life calling and would always be my major identity.

Yet shortly after my daughter was born, my lifelong passion for understanding human behavior, relationships, and psychology intensified. I felt growing within me a deep stirring, a powerful intuition that this, too, was somehow meant to be an important part of my life work. As a result, I felt a deep inner calling to go back to graduate school, to earn a master's degree in counseling psychology. Everyone I knew was quite surprised, always having thought of me solely as an artist...and now...*what* was I...*who* was I?

I struggled with the question of how to reconcile these two different career interests. For a time, I thought perhaps it was necessary to give up one major aspect of myself in order to access and develop another. One day I gave away all my art supplies to a friend, thinking I would not be using them anymore, as visual art was no longer my major pursuit. Yet several years later, after that night of the guided visualization, I began to open to a new awareness. I realized more fully than ever this truth:

We are all many selves. We each have numerous important aspects to who we are...and we can honor and respect each of them, and we can find ways to invite them ALL to be present in our lives. We can weave together the fabric of our most magnificent selves from the beautiful threads of many of the unique and wondrous colors of our life's experiences, our gifts, talents, strengths, and joys...and we are so much the richer and stronger for it...

I then saw that I did not have to relinquish who I had been in order to accept who I was now becoming. I could indeed have many identities at once, as can we all. I could be a mother, an artist, a writer, a teacher, a healer, a seeker of truth and spirit, and a creator of beauty, all woven into one integrated self. My particular way of combining all of these elements together would be a unique one. Yet I would somehow find a way to make it all work—and I am still now in the process of so doing, as my pathway continues to further unfold.

Realizing and honoring the many aspects of who *you* are—and allowing each of them to rise to the surface—is a vital part of your quest of self-discovery too. This quest also requires that you take the time, every day, to tune into your own inner voice, to listen for the truths within that are deeply embedded in your heart and soul. And you must prepare to be open and willing to follow the messages that you do receive, even when it means you must make changes in your life—and even when they are major ones.

That voice calling to you from within
is your ever-present intuition...
and yet you must sometimes cut through
heavy layers of doubts, fears, and confusion
to access it, to hear your soul's wisdom, which
wants to whisper gently to you your own truths,
which will lead you to wise decisions, right choices...

If you can enter the silence within
and trust the process, know that no matter
the problem or question or challenge before you,
in good time the answers you await will come...
Clarity will be your partner...
and the pathway will open before you...

Our deepest wishes
are whispers of our authentic selves.
We must learn to respect them.
We must learn
to listen

Sarah Ban Breathnach

The *Mirror of Truth and Intuition* now asks you to reflect upon the following questions:

You have many selves, many important aspects of who you are. Are there some that are calling out to you to be recognized and more fully developed?

Which of your identities are of greatest importance to you right now? Which ones might become stronger for you in the future?

When do you feel that you are accessing and living your deepest truths? What can you do to bring this about more often?

What is the most important message that your intuition is giving you right now? Are you willing to listen to it?

Have there been times in your life when you have listened to your intuition? What have some of the results been?

When have you not followed your intuition and later regretted it? What have you learned from this? Can it move you toward taking your intuition more seriously now?

5.

The Mirror of Creativity

Acclaiming
Your Creativity
& Unique Gifts

Essentially we are all creative beings, manifesting our creativity daily in a multitude of ways...

& We are all far more gifted, more creative, more inventive & more imaginative than we realize...

Caroline Joy Adams

You Are a Woman Finding and Using Your Creativity and Unique Gifts...

As we learn to seek our own deep truths, and listen more closely to our intuition, such careful listening cannot help but move us in the direction of finding and accessing our true gifts—those areas in life in which our creativity can take shape, grow, and blossom most richly. For essentially we are *all* creative beings, manifesting our creativity daily in a multitude of ways—and we are all far more gifted, more creative, more inventive, and more imaginative than we ever realize.

Every single day, even though you do not always think of it like this, you are exercising your *own* inherent creativity in at least a dozen different ways. Every time that you cook a meal, you are engaged in a highly creative act, a vital form of artistic expression. Every positive communication you initiate with someone is a creative act, especially when it serves to bring about a greater depth of understanding and love. Your efforts to create a home that reflects your unique sense of beauty are ever-unfolding creative acts. And you undoubtedly bring your creativity to your work every day, even if in small and sometimes subtle ways.

For creativity, in whatever form, is about having a vision and taking the actions to bring it into being...

Creativity abounds—it exists everywhere, and is in all of us, all the time. To be alive is to be a human being in the continual process of creation...

Some of us were fortunate enough to have been encouraged early on to access and celebrate our innate creativity: to sing, dance, make art or music, or otherwise be fully present in our most joyous, spontaneous, creative selves. Far too often, however, such nurturing of our creative instincts was not the case—and it is much later along the pathways of our lives that we can even begin to allow them to flow forth and come to life.

Many of us are still totally immersed in this process. We are searching and seeking and finding out what our truest calling is, discovering what our greatest gifts are, those that call forth our deepest capacities and greatest pleasures, those that allow us to truly and finally flourish to our fullest extent.

The process is an ongoing one and takes much experimenting, exploring, and expanding of our sense of what is possible. Sometimes our most important creative avenues result from a great mixture of talent and technique, instinct and intuition. And while some forms of creative expression may come easily to us, others may require many years of intense practice and great patience before we achieve a sense of accomplishment and expertise.

I know that I am continually awakening to ever-deeper layers of my own creative powers. But developing my creative gifts and artistry has by no means been an easy road. Instead, it continues to be one with many deep struggles along the way. What amuses me at times is how people sometimes react when watching me write so easily with a colorful marker in my free-flowing calligraphic style—such as when I am in a store writing out a check in this way. They often comment on how lucky I am to have such beautiful handwriting. I smile, thinking they imagine that this particular talent perhaps came to me naturally and effortlessly.

Nothing could be further from the truth. When I was eighteen, and discouraged about my nearly illegible handwriting, I discovered a calligraphy instruction manual in my college bookstore. I decided to teach myself from it, and worked hard to imitate its letter models. Pleased with my progress, I kept at it for the next few years.

What I didn't know was that the book itself had been written by someone whose own skill in this art form was not very highly developed. And so my own style, copied from poor-quality letter models, was actually quite awkward and unattractive to look at.

Five years later I finally realized this truth, after obtaining a job at a calligraphy studio in New York City, where I lived at the time. There we spent long hours each day inscribing names on certificates and awards in a variety of intricate calligraphic styles. Before long I noticed, to my dismay, that most of my coworkers were actually far more skilled than I was. Their work had a certain grace and flow, a sense of beauty and balance that mine clearly lacked. I then found out that they had all attended the nearby Cooper Union School of Art, where they had studied calligraphy with a master teacher—and had received a foundation that I had altogether missed.

Finally able to see the difference between their highly refined letter-shapes and my own, I knew I had to go straight back to the beginning. I began using copies of the instruction sheets my fellow workers had received from their excellent teacher. I practiced diligently many hours a day, in a new state of heightened awareness about what I was trying to achieve. Still, it took a year or two to get to a much higher level of skill. And it was another seven years before I developed what can now be recognized as my own colorful and unique style of this art form.

Fully accessing my own creativity has certainly been a challenging task all along—and still is, each and every day. Yet I have come to strongly believe that it is the challenges themselves that also make it possible for me to bring forth my greatest gifts and creative expressions. And I imagine that in whatever unique ways you channel your *own* creative instincts, this may well be true for you, too.

As you now look into the *Mirror of Creativity*, it is time for you to begin to acknowledge the many ways you have already begun to bring *your* gifts and creativity into being. Especially if you have not thought of yourself as the gifted, creative person whom I know you to be, here are some questions to contemplate:

What are some of the most significant ways that you are now expressing your creativity? Are you reaching a greater awareness of your own deepest gifts and beginning to use them to a greater extent?

What are you in the process of creating that is most important to you?

What are all the smaller, yet still very real ways that you are also engaging in creative acts on a daily basis?

How do you feel when you are at your most creative?

6.

The Mirror of Passion & Power

Recognizing

Your Power that Arises from Within

the source of continuing
Aliveness is to
find your passion
& pursue it with whole heart
& single mind!

Gail Sheehy

You Are a Woman Finding Your Passions in Life and Sensing Your Power That Arises from Within...

In the process of realizing your true gifts, you will inevitably find both your deepest passions and your greatest sense of power. For your unique gifts are those capacities which, when exercised to the fullest, make you feel excited, exhilarated, energized—unbridled, unlimited, unrestrained. This is the place where true passion lies, and where true power resides, and is able to be accessed most readily.

What is it that you are now in most passionate pursuit of? Is it daring to bring a dream alive that has simmered beneath the surface within you for years, awaiting your readiness to bring it into being? Is it manifesting a vision for your life, your work, your family, your relationships? Is it your desire to give birth to a child, a new career, or perhaps a new aspect of yourself that has lain dormant but is now about to magnificently unfold? What is it that ignites your passion...and where is it leading you now?

As Gail Sheehy states in *New Passages*, "The source of continuing aliveness is to find your passion, and pursue it with whole heart and single mind!"

And what about *power*? That very word evokes deep feelings in most of us. What does it really mean? Among the definitions found in *Webster's Dictionary* are these: "the capacity or ability to do or accomplish something; a particular ability, capability, or skill." I believe that the majority of women resonate with these definitions, for the *power from within* that we long to possess more of is represented for most of us by a capacity to accomplish something, that we may feel increasingly positive about ourselves and confident in our abilities.

When do you personally feel your sense of power rising from within? For many of us, consideration of this question brings us to the realization that we unfortunately don't feel our most capable, confident, powerful selves all that often. So take some time to think about this. When *do* you really feel your sense of power? What brings it about most potently for you? What is it like for you when you are, even fleetingly, immersed in that feeling?

I believe that many of us today are discovering our true passions in life, and are beginning to take the steps to pursue them. We are also accessing, one moment at a time, that sense of power that allows us to feel most centered in the core of who we are. Yet this does not come easily to most of us—which is why I find the words of Della Reese a helpful reminder: "Get firmly planted in, relaxed in, comfortable in your power. Don't ever be afraid to use it. Be proud you have it, and use it every chance you get."

Over the past five years, I've gradually learned to access my own sense of power from within more often. I am still not able to do this all the time, by any means—but at least I find I can do so more consistently than I used to. I am working towards the day when I will be able to feel present in my power more often still. And I have a strong intuition that you are also moving in this direction—in your own way, and in your own time.

Yet sometimes it seems that traveling first through the darkness is essential in order to emerge, reborn, into the radiant light of our personal power. This rebirthing of ourselves is something we women seem to be called upon to experience over and over again. I personally find my own yearly birthdays to be a time when I like to reflect on where I now am, and where I have been. Recently, I realized that comparing two such occasions, a few years apart, most clearly demonstrates my tangible progression over time.

Four years ago, as I approached my upcoming birthday, I had an inner sense that the year ahead would be a significant one, that thirty-five was to be for me an empowering age. I was not sure exactly how this would manifest, as I was still living on a daily basis in a very difficult circumstance, in a deeply troubled marriage that I was not yet willing to give up hope on. My daily life seemed an endless stream of demands, from my

Get firmly planted in,
relaxed in, comfortable
in your power
Don't ever be afraid to
use it... Be proud you
have it... & use it
every chance you get...

Della Reese

husband to my business to my young daughter. My real hope was that somehow things would get easier, and that feeling more in touch with my power would perhaps go hand in hand with feeling more in control of my daily life.

Instead, just the opposite happened. Six weeks before my thirty-fifth birthday, my husband suddenly left us. Reeling in shock and pain and grief, it was all I could do to get through each day, trying, though not always successfully, to hold back the torrent of tears that wanted to flood forth in every moment. I did not want my daughter to become frightened and overwhelmed at seeing me in such a state of sadness. Those first few months were by far the roughest, and in the midst of them came my birthday—which I hardly felt was worthy of celebration.

What I chose to do was to attend an all-day women's retreat at a local spiritual center. It was hard for me to even find the energy to go, knowing I would see people there who had known me in what now felt like another lifetime, and I would have to reveal the painful truth about my new life circumstance. Yet I felt it might be a positive, healing environment at the same time, so I forced myself to make the arrangements to attend. I dropped my daughter off at my sister's house, hoping she would fare well that day also.

Halfway through the day, I called to check on her. The news was not what I wanted to hear—no, the answer came, she was not doing well—*not at all*. She seemed to have saved up her own rage, fear, and grief, her deep distress at her father's leaving, and was releasing it full force that day, in raging sobs and fits of temper directed at my sister, and even at her young cousin, whom she normally adored. Perhaps afraid and unable to release her emotions in my presence, not wanting to upset me further, she felt more free to let loose her own flood of feelings in my absence.

I will never forget the feeling that overcame me that day as I hung up the phone, alone in the office of the retreat center. I, too, broke into sobs, uncontrollable ones. I felt like this was it—the sign that no, she was not all right, I was not all right, *nothing would ever, ever be all right with our lives, ever again*. She was as emotionally devastated as I was, though she'd been trying in her beautiful, innocent, five-year-old way to be on her best behavior by hiding her own intense pain from me.

But there was no longer any place to hide. The pain was so deep—it seemed chasmic, infinite, threatening to overwhelm both of us. I could not see how I would ever be able to make up for this terrible loss in her young life, or how I would ever be able to go on and rebuild the shattered pieces of our lives. If I could not even spend a day away from her without her also falling to pieces emotionally, how would we ever even be able to begin the process of creating new lives for ourselves?

For what was probably half an hour, yet seemed like an eternity, I just sat down and let the tears finally come. I cried for myself, for my shattered dreams. I cried for my daughter, who would now grow up not knowing what it is like to have a loving father present. I cried for all the women and children the world over who also know this very specific and deepest pain from their own personal experience. Finally, I pulled myself together enough to return to the group. At day's end, I went and picked up my daughter, and took her home, and we wept together—all that evening, and on and on, into that dark night of the soul.

That summer was one of great despair. I stopped caring about almost everything for a time, and even considered giving up the business of *Inspirations*, feeling that it, too, was more than I could cope with. For who was I, awash in my own grief, to write inspiring words for others?

But little by little, the light returned, and the grief and tears lessened. By summer's end, I had major decisions to make, and I needed strength to make them. One such decision was where to live. The house that we had lived in as a family was now much too large and expensive for me to afford on my own. I knew I had to move, and I agonized for a couple of months as to where—and as to how I would pay for it. And my daughter was going to enter kindergarten in the fall, and I had to find a good school environment for her.

For several years by then, my business had been home-based, and in every place we had lived, had begun to take over the house. Every surface seemed to be covered, overflowing with all the materials necessary to get the merchandise together to ship to the stores. Countless boxes of frames, prints, and magnets were everywhere, with endless piles of paperwork scattered in their midst. It felt like there was never any escaping from the chaos of it all.

One of the best and most empowering decisions I have ever made came that fateful summer. One day, desperate for a break from my daughter, I had a babysitter take her off for a few hours. It was then, in that moment of aloneness, that I came to a life-altering insight. I realized that it was time to get the business out of the house. It was time to declare it as a real business, one that would actually take up space in the world. This would give me a place to go to outside the home each day where I could expand, at last, this important aspect of my life.

The real task before me was nothing less than totally reinventing my life, in every aspect—and so I took the first major concrete steps forward. I found us a new home, a small yet pleasant apartment in the center of a small town with a good school system, not far away. Best of all, it was only a five-minute drive from a renovated old factory building that had been converted into office space, where I could finally have a professional, spacious place in which to work.

The large house that I moved from had been set deep in the woods, and had been a terribly lonely and isolating place to be after my husband's departure. My physical move to a new place felt quite symbolic of my coming out of the woods and into a place of clearing and light. In this new landscape, I could feel the dark clouds lifting, and could begin to sense the beauty of life and possibilities for the future opening to me once again.

Moving my business out into the world was also significant. It then began to grow in a much more dramatic way—and so did I, in the process.

My thirty-fifth year began in what felt like a tragic shattering of all that I had ever known—certainly not a place of empowerment. Yet by its end, I had shifted into a new place, both physically and spiritually. As difficult as it was to adjust to living on my own, I was beginning to feel a sense of actual gratitude that I was now free from the daily pain of living with someone who could not honor who I was.

As I think now about my journey of these past few years, I see how far I have come. This past June, during the week of my most recent birthday, I chose to attend a five-day seminar in Los Angeles, three thousand miles from home. The topic of this course was how to come into a much greater awareness of one's life purpose, personal power, and inner and outer resources. There were about a hundred people present, including my daughter, whom I proudly brought along. Now a calm, centered child, very much at ease with adult company, she delighted my classmates with her presence.

At dinnertime, I stood up and announced that it was my birthday, and the room resounded with a spontaneous chorus of a hundred beautiful voices wishing me a "Happy Birthday," which it surely was. Just the fact that I *could* be present, truly present, with these hundred souls, fellow travelers on the pathway to self-discovery, felt like a great gift in itself. As a way of giving thanks that I was at last in a place where I could once again celebrate life—and my own birthday as part of it—I gave each person a gift, one of my *Inspirations* prints.

This is what I believe power is really about: being fully present with yourself and with others...becoming aware of your gifts...fully acknowledging, developing, and utilizing your highest capacities...and finding new and wonderful ways to share them with others!

Take a look now into the *Mirror of Passion and Power*. Take some time to reflect on your own experiences of accessing your source of power from within—and consider as well your experience of finding and pursuing your passions. For at each new life stage, new treasures and new discoveries of who we are make themselves known to us. Each new life phase may bring forth new and deeper aspects of our personal sense of power—and new passions, gifts, dreams, and visions to explore.

What moments can you recall in your life when you have felt your most capable, when your inner core of personal power has been most present?

Think back in time, if you wish, perhaps to five or ten years ago. What aroused this feeling of power for you then, compared to what does so now?

What current activities bring you most in touch with this feeling? What can you do to experience this feeling of being at your strongest and most capable more and more often? What would have to change in your life, work, relationships, or family for this to happen, and how would it feel?

What are the things in your life that you feel most passionate about? Have they changed over time? Are they related to your greatest gifts and talents?

Are there ways in which you can devote yourself more fully to these things, even one small step at a time?

7.

The Mirror of Yourself in Relation to Others

Becoming Aware

of the Ways Your Presence Makes a Difference to Others

We are all here
to be of service
to one another...
& One soul, gracing anothers life,
one moment at a time, is what
Life, essentially, is all about...

Caroline Joy Adams

You Are a Woman Whose Presence
Touches the Lives of Others in Significant Ways...

Our journey of self-recognition is now about to expand as we look into the mirror that reflects your presence in the lives of others. For the continually unfolding, always sacred journey of your life is about many things, including: learning to love yourself and others as compassionately as possible, growing more deeply into your own inner wisdom, expanding more fully into who you are, sharing your gifts with others, and, in the process, being of true service to others along the way.

We are all here to be of service to one another...
to grace one another's lives with offerings of our skills and
talents, our time and energy, our resources, and our love...

Just as you are weaving a magnificent tale of your own life, at
the same time you are playing a significant, sometimes
powerfully influential role in the life stories of others...
For you are at once a student of life and love and a teacher...

And we are all here to be both teachers and students, fellow
healers, dreamers, companions to one another on the
pathway...We are here, essentially, to be mirrors for one
another's souls...and to bring beauty, healing, and
light to one another's hearts...

Even though each of us, on the grand cosmic scale of the universe, can only make what may seem to be a small difference, the truth is that small things, when done with great love, can *become* great things. And the small acts that we contribute to each other—the ones of connection, grace, beauty, understanding, and love—are the ones that truly matter.

For one soul, gracing another's life, one moment at a time, is what life, essentially, is all about. I came to this realization some dozen years ago. At a time when I was feeling that my work was not of any great value to anyone, I was then told otherwise, by one wise and special soul, in the form of a letter that forever changed my perspective. How I wish I still had that letter. It has unfortunately long since been lost, yet its message, now embedded deeply within my heart, will never be forgotten.

While in an earlier stage of finding my life work, for a time I enjoyed making a living as an artist with a specialty in calligraphy. But after several years, I had inscribed thousands upon thousands of anonymous names of people I would never meet on diplomas, name cards, and envelopes, and my work began to feel quite tedious. Most of the time I felt a deep and growing sense of restlessness, of discontent. It seemed that what I was doing was just not important. I yearned to feel that I was making a real difference to others, but could not feel, or believe, that this was true.

But I did have one way to experience a wonderful sense of connection to others through my work. For several years, I spent every Wednesday evening teaching a calligraphy class at Harvard University—and indeed, this was the highlight of my week. My students, taking courses through the adult education division, were a wide mix of ages and backgrounds, and I loved teaching them to make letters come alive and to access their own creativity and artistic gifts.

Since I found few worthwhile textbooks on calligraphy that I could use for my classes, I decided to write one. For the next year, I poured my heart and soul into the creation of an in-depth instruction book on Italic, my favorite calligraphic style. It was then published by a small art book publisher. The day the first finished copies were delivered to me was a momentous occasion—and I celebrated soon afterwards by throwing a publication party at a downtown Boston bookstore-café owned by a friend.

Over time, though, it became painfully clear that few people actually buy calligraphy textbooks. And so commercial success was just not the destiny of that book. Although a British paperback edition fared somewhat better in Europe, within a couple of years after its release the book was no longer to be found on bookstore shelves in this country, and was never reprinted. I had created the book more as a labor of love than with any great expectation of monetary rewards. But it was still discouraging to feel that all of my efforts had been of such seemingly little use.

Yet one day, two years later, I received a large manila envelope addressed to me in a strong, spirited, calligraphic hand, forwarded by my publisher. I opened it with great curiosity. To my surprise, the writer was a young man who eloquently explained that he had been going through a terrible time in his life, and had been deeply depressed, to the point of considering suicide.

He had then found my calligraphy book, and began teaching himself the art of beautiful writing by using it. He had made astounding progress, as evidenced by the lovely examples of his work enclosed with his letter. Due to his newfound excitement at having found an art form through which he could express himself creatively, his life had now taken a significant turn for the better. In deep gratitude, he wanted to let me know that my book had been instrumental in helping him believe in himself once again—and, so he felt, had actually helped save his life.

I was amazed—I had long resigned myself to the belief that creating that book had simply been a learning experience for me, with no tangible results for anyone else. But this letter changed my thinking forever. I realized that even if my year's effort had affected only one person in a deep way, that was actually enough. Had I not received that letter, I never would have known of the effect of my work on this one kindred soul. For the truth is that we are all continually creating such effects on each other's lives, though often unknowingly. Those we are close to and those we may have never even met are deeply affected by our words, our actions, our presence, our love, and our work.

Small things
when done with
great love
become great things

Caroline Joy Adams

Your Work Touches the Lives of Others Every Day

We are now going to think about some important ways that your presence touches the lives of others. First, we will consider the work you have done, and how it affects others—for work is such a deeply important aspect of each of our life journeys.

As a vital part of your own life quest, you, too have undoubtedly been searching, seeking, and striving to find just what type of work makes best use of your unique talents and energies.

Perhaps you have finally found work you love, and are devoting yourself to it fully, or you may be in a stage of preparation to do so. Or you may still be in a process of discovering just what your greatest interests and abilities are, and don't quite know where the search may eventually lead.

Yet whether your work is a temporary job or your impassioned life mission, it inherently *is* of service to the lives of many others. Your work contributes to their lives—and to the world—in direct and indirect ways. This is true for all of us, even when we don't *feel* that our work is important or highly valued in the world.

For it takes all of the diverse skills and talents of all of us to do the work of the world that needs to be done each day. And it is quite fortunate that we do each have different talents and strengths, which we can each contribute in our own unique ways.

Take some time now to honor and acknowledge the positive effects that your work has had in the world—and is having right now—by contemplating the following questions.

What are some of the many ways in which the various jobs you have held have been of service to others—even those that have not felt particularly creative or fulfilling at the time?

Who are some of the people whose lives you have touched through your work in the past—and whose lives you are touching right now?

How has the search for fulfilling work helped you discover more of who you are?

If You Are a Mother, Your Very
Important Work Touches the Lives of So Many

It may be that your time and energies have been—or now are—mostly devoted to the extremely important and immensely challenging work of mothering. If so, you are offering nurturing, teaching, healing, and deepest love not only to your own children, but to all whose lives are in turn affected by their wonderful presence in the world.

You are also part of an incredibly important shift in human history. For we are now realizing the tremendous importance of treating children—their feelings, and their needs, at all developmental stages—with deep respect. We are doing our best to bring up boys to be far more aware of their feelings and in touch with their loving essence than ever before—so they may one day become men who are infinitely capable of creating loving, respectful relationships when they become husbands and fathers.

At the same time, we are bringing up our daughters, from their earliest years, to be far more aware of both their inner and outer strengths. We are instilling in them the self-confidence that will allow them to go forth on their own life journeys with a continual sense of themselves as strong, intelligent, capable beings, able to accomplish great things.

As a mother, your devotion to raising sons and daughters of great gentleness, spirit, and strength has enormous import for the entire future of humanity. And this work of mothering is about the most difficult and challenging that many of us will ever do. Yet it is not always easy to see the immediate rewards of our labor, especially when our children are facing challenges of their own, at any given life stage. But please take a moment to silently acknowledge yourself, right now, for all the immense efforts you have made to be the very best mother that you can be. This huge, all-consuming task of guiding and nurturing others is work of the most complex, life-changing, and significant kind—and you deserve to be honored for your dedication to it, to the highest degree.

Look deeply now into the *Mirror of Yourself in Relation to Others*, as you ask yourself these questions about how your presence has positively affected others in the world.

Who are the people whose lives you have touched most deeply? (These may include family members, friends, coworkers, students, or others.)

How have you changed, transformed, guided, or influenced them in positive ways by your presence in their lives? How have you shaped their experiences or life paths?

What have they been able to bring forth within themselves that they may never have discovered without your encouragement and support?

Now take a few moments to imagine each of these people. Hold them close to your heart, and think about how *their* life journey has unfolded, and what your role has been. Think of the many ways you have expressed love to them, the ways you have been of greatest service in their awakening to their own highest self, the gifts you have given that have allowed each of them to access their own greatest gifts.

For I want you to begin remembering who you really are…and just how beautiful and important a presence you are in this world, all the time. I hope that you will take the time to write down some of your responses to the questions posed in this mirror. The answers will await you, whenever you seek a reminder of who you are and how you serve to positively transform the lives of others.

As fellow travelers on the journey of life, we are here to give and receive our greatest gifts to and from one another—and that is what makes the journey worthwhile for all.

Part Two.

The Seven Pathways to Celebrating Who You Are

Without
understanding
there cannot be true
LOVE
And without love there cannot
be true understanding...

— Thich Nhat Hanh

The Journey from
Understanding to Love to Celebration

I hope you have now begun to discover some of the many rich treasures of the continually evolving, beautiful being that you are—and who you are exists on three essential, interconnected levels at once. At your core level is a luminous, radiant *spirit,* or soul—which is housed in your *body,* that miraculous and remarkable vehicle that carries you through your days and nights and is capable of experiencing incredible pleasure, intense pain, and everything in between.

Just as marvelous and intricate is the third element of your self, your individual, creative *mind,* which stores a stunning array of your vast and varied life experiences, your perceptions, and, on both conscious and subconscious levels, your moment-to-moment thoughts and feelings. When mind, body, and spirit work together in greatest harmony, you can truly become the magnificent person you are meant to be. In such moments you are most capable of consciously creating a life that is a distinct and majestic expression of your highest self.

For you are here on earth at this time of great transition and transformation because you have a very special purpose in this lifetime, a unique and marvelous mission to fulfill. There is so much you have done, and are doing right now, that cannot possibly be done by anyone else. *Who you are matters:* your life matters, your work matters, your relationships to others matter; the examples you set daily, of courage and resilience, compassion and kindness, matter. Your moments of joy and of triumph matter.

You are also here on a learning journey. And the most important lessons for each one of us—although we may be at different stages of learning along the pathway—are the ones about *love.*

Love is deeply intertwined with *understanding*, for understanding is truly the essential companion to—and the very ground of—real love. As Thich Nhat Hanh, the inspiring writer and teacher, says in *Living Buddha, Living Christ*, "Without understanding there cannot be true love, and without love there cannot be true understanding." In the same book, he also says, "When you touch deep understanding and love, you are healed."

Love, essentially, is the desire to truly understand,
honor, and respect the feelings and experiences of another...
to see, through the eyes of compassion, who they really are, in
all of their unique imperfections and vulnerabilities,
as well as their strengths...

Love is about paying attention,
looking deeply, listening with reverence...and about
expressing the greatest caring and kindness...

Love is also much more than a feeling. It is indeed
a call to action, a call to continually and consciously take the
actions that can create more joy, inner peace, and
contentment for those whom you love...
moment by moment, day by day...

You have been looking at your own life here as a way to gain an awareness of yourself as the wise, courageous, and creative woman that you are. Reaching an increased understanding of our past experiences—and of our greatest needs, wishes, and *present* desires—allows us to come to *love* ourselves more. And learning to loving ourselves—and those around us—is essentially what we are all here to do.

With this growing self-awareness, this increased clarity of mind, we can then take the appropriate actions to show great care and kindness toward ourselves. At the same time, our ability to bring joy and peace into the minds, hearts, and lives of others becomes greatly enhanced. We can then extend ourselves toward others from an inner well of love that is full, one that is richly, freely, infinitely flowing.

We have now come full circle, from understanding to love to celebrating who we are! So let us now explore some of the many ways to begin to celebrate ourselves more fully, each and every day. The word *celebrate* actually has many possible meanings. The one I like best is "to *rejoice* in"—which means *to take delight in*, and *to cause joy to*. This involves many new ways of thinking, of being, and of seeing. These can make powerful, positive, and permanent differences in how you experience your daily life.

Each of the Seven Pathways to Celebrating Who You Are will enable you to express greater caring and love toward yourself and others, thus creating more moments of peace, fulfillment, inner satisfaction, and joy in your life. My hope is that you will invite some of them into your daily life, expand upon them, and find that your entire life can become a continual, never-ending pathway of celebration.

When you entered this world, long ago, your birth was a time of celebration and joy. It is now time to return to the joy, the wonder, the beautiful core essence of who you are, and to immerse yourself in the clear, healing waters of celebration once again.

1.

The Pathway of Nurturing

Nurturing

Yourself More Fully Each Day

Go deep
inside yourself
Find that treasure
that is known by
your name...

Virginia Satir

You Are Finally Learning to Truly Love and Nurture Yourself....

The first pathway is one of learning to nurture ourselves more fully, by beginning to treat ourselves with all the kindness and loving care that we normally bestow on others. It is time now for all of us to take these wonderful words of Virginia Satir to heart: "Go deep inside yourself. Find that treasure that is known by your name."

Many of us have been reaching a heightened state of awareness about taking care of ourselves, and are coming to treasure aspects of ourselves in new ways. We are beginning to pay more attention to our bodies, we are recognizing the importance of eating healthful food and engaging in exercise, and we are starting to do both more consistently. At the same time, we are making significant strides forward in other areas. We are working toward creating healthier relationships that nurture others as well as ourselves; we are taking the time to work on serious psychological issues; we are exploring and deepening our spiritual lives; and we are making time to do more of the things we enjoy, occasionally even allowing ourselves to spend money on small luxuries that bring us great pleasure.

Over the course of the past few years, I have been trying to stay much more clearly and consciously on this pathway myself. Although it is a constant challenge to take the time and energy to do so, I am glad that I am finally making the effort. My own list of self-nurturing activities grows all the time, and includes, among other things: receiving a relaxing massage, listening to music that I love, composing my own free-flowing melodies on my electronic keyboard, going out to eat with a friend or my daughter, and daily meditation and prayer, especially when I take unhurried time for this important act of self-renewal.

In addition, very high on my list is something I rarely did at all until this past year: *travel*. I will never forget the first summer after my husband was gone. It was so hard for me even to make my way down to the local lake to go swimming on those stiflingly hot August days. The sight of children playing happily with their devoted fathers, knowing those families were whole, together, complete—and mine never would be again—was so painful I just couldn't bear experiencing it.

Fortunately, time has given me courage, healing, and new perspectives. This past summer, I was ready to travel, not only on occasion to the local swimming spot, but much further still—halfway around the world, in fact. This was my way of declaring that yes, I have traveled far upon my own healing pathway—I *can* have a vision and bring it into reality—and I deserve to give my daughter and myself a spectacular experience. I decided to fulfill a lifetime fantasy of going to Hawaii, not for the romance I had always imagined, but as a marvelous adventure for a mother and daughter who can now proudly venture forth into the world complete in themselves and content in each other's company.

For five glorious late summer days, we toured the lush green islands. We hiked up mountain trails, listening to the wondrous, vibrant sounds of the glistening rain forest, teeming with life. We immersed ourselves in the incredibly warm, clear, blue-green waters of the spectacular sea that spread out before us, silken, inviting, jewel-like. The gentle, healing waves washed over our bodies, soothing our very souls. We stood in awe at the edge of an ancient, dormant volcano, sipped creamy pineapple-coconut cocktails, and ate chocolate-covered macadamia nuts to our hearts' content.

Barefoot, we strolled for miles each evening along the beach, feeling the cool, moist sand between our toes with each step. From glorious sunset to the shimmering moonlight, on and on into the deliciously fragrant tropical evenings we walked, gazing up at the spectacular sky above, ablaze with thousands upon thousands of radiant stars, brilliantly lighting up our pathway...

You, too, deserve to walk freely upon this nurturing pathway—and have undoubtedly begun to take important steps in that direction.

Consider the specific ways that you have already started to treat yourself with greater care and love, whether they focus on mind, body, spirit—or all three at once, as is often the case. At the same time, ask yourself this: What *new* nurturing activities would you now like to invite into your life?

This might mean taking more time for yourself, even half an hour per day or per week. Perhaps you would like to make an appointment with a massage therapist, to soothe both body and soul, or to take a hot herbal bath, with candles lit and soft music to listen to as you luxuriate, even for a brief interlude, in the warm, healing waters. Or would taking a weekend trip— to the ocean, the mountains, or a nearby or distant city—to relax or explore some new sights be a nurturing experience for you?

And what can you do to celebrate and nurture the miraculous gift of your body? Can you become more conscious of eating foods that truly nurture and sustain you, such as whole grains and vibrantly colored fresh fruits and vegetables? Can you take a dance class, begin to go for long walks— or engage in another form of regular exercise or healing work that focuses on the body?

At times you may just want to treat yourself to something purely pleasurable, healthy or not. One of my own favorite and frequent personal pastimes is to take a trip to a well-stocked local bookstore, browse for hours on end, and then buy an enticing new book or two. I then love to relax in an adjacent café. Slowly sipping a mocha-flavored milkshake, savoring some fresh-baked cookies, my crisp new books in hand—I am close to heaven!

Wearing just the right clothing can also make us feel wonderful. I love to put on velvet or silk as often as possible, with purple, royal blue, or emerald green hues. This type of clothing can instantly make me feel more attractive and alive. If you wish to and you can, go shop for a new dress or a silky nightgown or scarf. Even an inexpensive new pair of earrings, a necklace, or bracelet can make you feel beautiful, sensual, and special.

You may also want to use some scented candles or essential oils, to take in the healing effects that aromatherapy has to offer. The scents of spearmint, orange spice, and almond are among my favorites of all, and seem to have immediate uplifting effects!

Surround yourself with the sights and scents of flowers and plants as often as you can. I try to have a beautiful bouquet of fresh flowers nearby whenever I can, to inspire me throughout the day, and open me to seeing and experiencing the ever-unfolding beauty of all life. If you enjoy gardening, consider creating this year an even more glorious garden than ever before, full of spectacular color, texture, and design that will delight your eyes and senses and bring beauty to others at the same time!

The possibilities are endless! Find those nurturing activities that appeal to you the most, and incorporate them into your life to a higher degree than ever before. Just imagine, if you were to make a commitment to engaging in at least two or three specific self-nurturing acts each day, how your whole day would be lived at a higher level of awareness, inner peace, and contentment.

Now ask yourself this: *What specific self-nurturing acts can you commit to that will truly make you feel special in the very near future, perhaps over the course of the week coming up? What will give you that luxurious feeling of taking good care of yourself, physically, emotionally, spiritually or otherwise?*

What about today? Is there something you can do for yourself this very day or evening that will give you a feeling of being especially nurtured?

And what about right now? Is there something small and simple that you can do this very moment to bring yourself some much-needed pleasure, comfort, or relaxation?

Whatever will enhance your sense of well-being, you deserve it...and you should find ways to treat yourself to such things, as often as you possibly can!

2.

The Pathway of Loving Speech

Speaking

to Yourself

in More Loving Ways

When we are able to
value our self-worth
as much as we listen to the self-critic
we begin to tap
the resource
of wisdom...

Angeles Arrien

You Are Learning to Speak to Yourself in a New Voice of Kindness and Respect...

One of the most important actions that we can take to express greater kindness to ourselves is to learn to speak to ourselves in a much more loving way. As much as possible, we need to learn to let go of that ever-present voice of self-doubt and fear that lives within us, which we all know only too well. Instead, we need to start replacing it, whenever we can, with an inner voice of self-respect and appreciation.

"When we are able to value our self-worth as much as we listen to the self-critic, we begin to tap the resource of wisdom," Angeles Arrien emphasizes in her book *The Four-Fold Way.* And in *Everyday Sacred,* Sue Bender says, "How we speak to ourselves can have a very powerful effect on what happens in our lives." This, too, is why we must begin to speak to ourselves in more affirmative ways than ever before.

Not that this is easy to do. Cultivating the art of using loving speech with ourselves is a wonderful goal, yet one that will probably take some very conscious, continual effort over time.

In this process, here is something that I have found most helpful: Create a list of every word that you can think of to describe yourself in a positive light. These can be words that describe your capacities, qualities, skills, or strengths—*even if you do not have them all the time,* but just occasionally. By realizing that the seeds of these marvelous qualities really do exist within us, we can water them, pay attention to them, and bring them forth. They can then grow and become much more clearly and consistently present within us.

Write out your own such list now, in a journal or notebook if you like, or perhaps on a beautiful piece of bordered stationery. Keep it in a special place, and look at it often! Or carry it with you, so that you can refer to it wherever you are, whenever you need a reminder of *who you truly are.*

Here are some sample words that may be appropriate for your list—and feel free to add many more. Expand your list continually, and you will find that each of these qualities will become expanded within you as well!

Radiant   Expressive   Affectionate
Ever-evolving   Energetic
Comforting Powerful Passionate Brave Discoverer Dancer
Dreamer Devoted Calm Courteous Gifted Spirited
Soulful Sweet Strong Sensual
Openhearted Playful Faithful Friend
Conscious Communicator Adventurous
Gentle Graceful Fiery Appreciative
Flourishing Alive Accomplished Growing
Beautiful Spirit   Healer of Hearts   Optimistic
Light-filled Joyous Compassionate Clear of Mind
Understanding Magnificent Gracious Generous
Warm   Wonderful   Wise
Kind Creative Courageous Enthusiastic

Now I invite you again to spend a few moments looking into a real mirror. Look deeply—with reverence and love—at the beautiful self that is reflected back to you. Take a few deep breaths and smile at yourself, smile from the very center of your being. Speak directly, and be aware of the true *tone* of your voice. Speak from the heart, infusing your voice with as much kindness as possible. Practice speaking *as if you are addressing the most honored guest who has ever graced your home.*

Begin with just a few words, perhaps using some of the wonderful descriptive words from your list. Give yourself messages of encouragement and acknowledgment. Or speak about a problem you are dealing with at present, and how you might best handle it. Speak out loud if you can, but silently if necessary, and allow yourself to take in and accept the positive feelings and messages that you are conveying. This may seem silly or awkward at first, but when you try it, you may just find that such self-talk can create an inner shift in how you think about and can then treat yourself.

By practicing for a brief time like this each day, you will soon be able to catch that voice of fear and doubt more and more often, and to transform it into the voice of kindness that you really need and want to hear. When you are able to speak to yourself in this way, it becomes far more likely that others will respond to you from this place and be able to speak to you more respectfully themselves.

Now ask yourself: *If you were to practice speaking in this new way right now, what are the most empowering statements that you could possibly make to yourself? What words can you say that will have a powerful and positive impact on how you move through the rest of this very day?*

Remember that you deserve to be treated, and spoken to, with caring, compassion, and genuine respect…by others and by yourself, all the time.

3.

The Pathway of Peace in the Moment

Creating

More Moments of Calm & Contentment Each Day

Peace
is present

right here & now, in ourselves & in everything we do & see... The question is whether or not we are in touch with it...

— Thich Nhat Hanh

You Are Learning to Touch
the Well of Peace That Lives Within You...

Life truly is a series of moments, one following another, day after day. Each new day, we are given the gift of approximately one thousand waking moments. What if we were to view each one as a new opportunity to learn to become as fully present—*and as peaceful*—as possible? As Thich Nhat Hanh says in *Peace Is Every Step,* "Peace is present right here and now, in ourselves and in everything we do and see. The question is whether or not we are in touch with it."

The ability to be totally present in the moment is one that most young children possess in abundance, which is why it can be such a joy to be around them. Their whole beings light up with such complete, spontaneous pleasure and enthusiasm when they are happy—and they usually experience many such moments each day. Yet as we grow up and the pressing concerns of everyday life begin to weigh upon us, slowly but surely we lose that ability to be truly and totally present. This shift away from being present in the moment, to focusing one's energy on the past or future, seems to begin even as young as age eight or nine.

As my daughter approaches her tenth birthday, I've noticed her losing her own spontaneity, as she begins to ask the deep and difficult questions about life, and her own unfolding future, that she would not have pondered quite so seriously a year or two ago. But in this particular week of time, as I write these words, she has been again experiencing more of the moment-to-moment joy of her former self. She is spending her days in the company of Nicholas, her favorite cousin, and Seth, an exuberant and special young eight-year-old friend from out of town who is visiting on his summer vacation.

These two boys, just slightly younger than she, are both still completely possessed of that infectious, marvelous ability to be completely and totally present in the moment. For now, they are bringing her back into that mode of being herself. Together the three of them are a lovely sight to behold, their eyes, faces, and very spirits sparkling with joy, spontaneity, laughter, and love. I feel blessed to be in their presence, to see this bright and delightful reminder of how wonderful it is to be so present, open, fully awake, and alive in the moment.

How rarely, though, we adults seem to be able to do so! Instead, so much of the time, our minds are at work lamenting the past, or worrying about the future and all that is not yet as we would wish it to be in our lives, judging ourselves and each other, mourning our losses, feeling frustrated at what we cannot control, and fearful of what could or might happen next. This river of continually flowing thoughts, perceptions, and the powerful and complex feelings that often accompany them seems never-ending.

At times, of course, we must fully *experience* the feelings that arise before we can let go and move beyond them. Feelings of sadness are certainly a normal and necessary response to the losses, large and small, that we all experience as we proceed through life. There are also times when anger and fear are justified, especially if we are being treated with disrespect or the anger of another is being directed towards us. These powerful emotions that we feel in response can warn us of potential danger, which we do need to recognize.

Yet even during our most difficult times, when it may seem impossible to experience a *general* sense of well-being, it may still be possible to create more *moments* in which we are fully present and experiencing a sense of inner peace. As time goes on, we can create more such moments still, until at last we arrive at a place where we are able to experience more moments of peace than moments of upset. *And this is the pathway of true healing.*

Whether we are in the midst of a challenging life phase, or simply facing a difficult situation on a given day, we *can* develop the ability to transform the uncomfortable emotions that take hold of us and create more moments of tranquillity. How can we begin to do this? To start with, we must develop a much greater moment-to-moment awareness of our thoughts and feelings *as they arise*. If we can first recognize our own feelings, and learn to remain relatively calm even under stressful circumstances, we will be much more able to make the sometimes difficult decisions that are necessary. This practice of gaining greater awareness and becoming more fully present in the moment, which may be referred to as *mindfulness*, can thus be helpful to us in all situations we encounter.

As soon as you notice uncomfortable emotions arising within you, see if you can stop, and become as conscious as you can of your thoughts, feelings, and perceptions. Then try to become aware of your breathing. If you can, take some deep, slow breaths. This can be very calming, and may help to return you to a state of equilibrium.

At the same time, you may wish to speak words to yourself that can transform difficult feelings into greater understanding, clarity, and peace. Choose a simple phrase to repeat in such situations, such as: *Clear mind, open heart.* Or find just one key word that you can easily remember, such as *harmony,* or *peace.* Anything that can return you to a greater sense of inner serenity is fine. By repeating your chosen phrase, breathing in the light of peace—and breathing out some of the tension that has arisen within—you will soon be able to let go of the *intensity* of the upsetting feeling. In this way, you may reach a greater state of calm before long—which will allow you to make much wiser choices about how to handle the situation that brought about the upset.

Mindfulness is also about becoming more fully *awake*. It is about learning to see anew the beauty of life that exists at all times—even while we confront sadness and suffering within the world and within ourselves. Although it is not always easy, I try to practice remaining aware and awake in the moment as much as I can throughout any given day. A few specific occasions in my life are etched in my memory as times when I realized most clearly the importance of this.

One such unforgettable occasion occurred on a July morning just two years ago. Just before darkness was about to break into light that day, I was awakened in a dramatic way. I arose to a terrible sound, emanating from our beloved animal companion, the beautiful five-year-old cat that both my daughter and I treasured greatly. She had become very ill, and now suddenly, right before our eyes, she was dying. Despite our frantic efforts to save her, within moments, the life was gone from her. Feeling helpless, in shock, and grief-stricken—after a time, we wandered out into our small front yard to catch our breath and begin to accept our loss, tears streaming down our faces.

In the meantime, the sun had risen, and the midsummer early morning light was incredibly beautiful, with that special luminous quality which is present shortly after dawn. I realized then how rarely I was awake at that time to witness this sight, and what I was missing. The light gave the entire yard a wondrous, almost mysterious glow. The tall green grass, delicious to the touch of our bare feet, was cool, wet, shining. The flowers in the garden displayed a magnificent array of colors—from lemon yellow to bright crimson to majestic purple to powdery blue—and an incredible variety of marvelous designs and intricate patterns. The leaves on the trees seemed to beckon to us, glistening with dew, and the birds were offering their sweet morning songs.

I had just suffered the loss of a great source of love and comfort to me, and my heart was heavy with sorrow. Yet incredible beauty still surrounded me—a beauty just as real and present as my grief. This realization seemed to cause the grief to lift briefly, and for a few moments, a profound sense of peace came over me. I have never forgotten that day or that feeling: it remains to me a powerful reminder to *awaken—to the beauty, magic, mystery, and wonder that are ever-present, all around us, if we can open our eyes to look—*even when grief and pain are present at the same time.

When I am in the midst of a greatly challenging time, I also find it useful to ask myself, as soon as I can, some soul-searching questions. If I can open to them fully, I have found the answers will always come, and work their transformative power over the depth of my thoughts and emotions. Here are a few of the questions that I try to remember to ask in my most difficult moments. Perhaps you, too, will find some of them helpful at times.

What if the exact event happening right now is here to allow me to open to a powerful life lesson, one that can facilitate my spiritual growth in a profound way? If so, just what is the "hidden gold" in this situation, and what is the greatest potential lesson for me here?

Am I being invited right now to become more flexible, patient, open-minded, compassionate, or lighthearted? What new awareness, skills, or qualities can this situation allow me to open to or to develop?

*Is it **helpful** right now for me to experience sorrow, anger, fear, frustration, hurt, or whatever else I am feeling? If it is, how can I transform this useful information into something that can lead me to make a wise choice in regard to the situation at hand?*

What can I do—right now—to best take care of myself, to return to a calm and clear state of mind, an open and loving heart?

I invite you to always remember that we do have the power within us to choose to transform, over and over again, our moments of upset into moments of insight—and then into moments of peace. It may be that you can only seem to do this occasionally at first. Yet with practice over the course of time, I am sure that you will be able to increase the number of moments each day that are lived in a state of calm, clarity, and contentment.

Eventually, this feeling of inner peace can become your natural state of being, almost all the time…and this, too, is an integral part of the pathway of celebrating who you are.

4.

The Pathway of Your Deepest Dreams

Taking Actions

Toward Making Your Dreams Come True

A few steps forward, a few steps back
Perhaps the purpose is not so much
to reach heaven, but to

Learn to
Dance
well...

Melanie Gendron

You Are in the Process of Manifesting
Your Greatest Life Visions and Dreams...

We have considered some ways to calm the mind and create inner peace, to appreciate the gifts and beauty of the present moment. At the same time, we *can* be completely aware of the important changes we may need to make, to ultimately live a life of great satisfaction and joy. But in order to create a life that is the richest, fullest expression of who we are, we first need to get a clear sense of just what our greatest visions and deepest dreams are. Next we must find the *essential elements* of those visions—and then we can begin to take the steps necessary to bring them about.

For everything begins with a vision, before it can manifest in material form. And some of our visions are so expansive, our dreams so detailed, that they may take dozens of steps, or many more still, over a very long time, to bring into being. Much patience is often required, as almost every worthwhile endeavor takes far longer and demands far more effort, energy, and endurance than we ever imagine. Keeping a clear vision of what is possible all along is paramount, so that we can persevere when our dreams take longer or are more difficult to bring into reality than we originally anticipated.

There are also many occasions in each of our lives when we have an original vision, a beautiful dream that we deeply cherish and believe for a time that we can bring to life. Yet we may then have to face the disappointing and sometimes devastating truth that what we most fervently desire just is not going to remain—or ever become—a reality. We may need to let go of something that we had thought we must have, or could never live without. This can happen when we lose someone of immense importance to us, through separation, divorce, or death. It may also be the case when we lose a job, a deep friendship, our physical health, our financial security, or anything else of great significance.

What happens then? First, we grieve. We mourn our losses, for we simply must experience the intense pain that loss brings, before we can begin to heal ourselves. If our loss is truly profound, our grieving continues on some level for the long term. Yet once we are past the first, most painful and difficult stages of the grief—which, depending on the nature of the loss, can take from several months to a number of years—we can begin to move on. This moving forward is almost always facilitated by our creating a new vision of something that is still possible to have in our lives in a very real way.

What I have found is that if we can search deeply within ourselves, and find the essence that represents the most treasured aspect of that lost dream, we can then open ourselves to new and expanded possibilities. And we may well be able to find a way to bring the dream about in a new and perhaps different form—one that can still bring great moments of joy and fulfillment to our lives.

I am still in the midst of this process myself, since various key elements of my own greatest dreams have not yet come to fruition. This includes a wholly respectful, committed relationship with a compatible life partner, and there are many moments when I have felt this lack deeply. But I have been open to exploring new relationships, and have learned a great deal in the process these last few years. And while I am not quite where I want to be in this aspect of my life, I am clear that all I have experienced is a superb training ground—a preparation for the time when all that is meant to be will blossom forth, and I will along with it.

I have also had to mourn the loss of the possibility of giving birth to a second child. My new dream is to adopt another child, to create a different, yet equally beautiful form of the expanded family I so long to have in my life. My daughter and I look forward to this future event, although it may be a way off, as adoption is a complex and often lengthy process.

At the same time, I have many other great dreams-in-progress. I want to write more books, to teach, to travel, to make connections with people all over the world. I want to live in a spacious, beautiful house, perhaps even one with a spectacular mountain or ocean view. My visions grow more expansive all the time, and I believe that someday many aspects of them, one by one, will indeed become reality.

Yet on the pathway to my dreams, I know that the following words, by Melanie Gendron, surely speak to my experience: "A few steps forward, a few steps back. Perhaps the purpose is not so much to reach heaven, but to learn to dance well." Perhaps you also resonate with this message, since this truly seems to be the way that most of us find that we move through life. For it may well be that learning to dance well—with the changes, challenges, and choices before us in each moment, on the pathway to making our dreams come true—really *is* our major life task.

The dance of life is a constant process, one of taking steps that lead us toward our dreams—and taking steps back...consciously creating, at times, what we can have, and accepting, at other times, that we cannot have what we most fervently want...letting go...and ultimately moving forward, once again, with an expanded awareness, a deepened sense of who we are and where we are going...

At times, we also need to ask ourselves some deep questions, in order to gain clarity and perspective on what our greatest dreams really are. In the past year or two I have done so myself, and one concrete result is the very book that you now hold in your hands. Although I enjoyed writing the inspirational phrases that I inscribe on my magnets and posters, my deepest wish was to greatly expand upon some of my favorite themes, perhaps to develop them into full-length books. But how could I bring this dream into reality, as I was already overburdened in terms of work and time? I imagined it would be at least five or ten years before I could find the time and energy that would need to be poured into such a huge project.

Yet not much more than a year ago, I came across a thought-provoking book entitled *A Year to Live,* which changed my thinking. It was written by

Stephen Levine, who, along with his wife, Ondrea, has worked for many years with those in the last stages of life. However, this book is not at all about dying. Instead, it is a call to live more fully and completely—*right now.* It asks you to imagine that you only had a year to live, and, if so, what you would wish to do with it. It raised questions like these: What would be the absolute best way to spend your last year of life, if you knew that was all you had left? With whom would you spend your time? What legacy would you most want to leave to the world? What would you want to feel that you had accomplished? What regrets would you have if you were to die today, if you did not live as fully as you might have?

These questions seeped into my soul, and stirred me to action. They caused me to consider whether I was using my gifts as fully as I could—or if perhaps something more, something greater, was being asked of me. The answer came to me rather quickly. *Yes*, I was meant to expand. I was to expand in every way—my capacities, my energy level, my sense of possibility, my connection to others, my vision. One part of this was to manifest my long-on-hold dream of expanding my writing into book form. Not five or ten or fifteen years down the road—but right away. Within weeks, I began work on this book, and have now cycled with it through the four seasons of this past year, changing and growing along with it each day, through each phase and moment of its creation.

Thus while some dreams must be put on hold, many others are calling out to us to be acted upon, right now, without delay, for we are being asked to bring forth the deepest expressions of who we are, at our essence...at each and every stage of our lives, in every possible way...

Do you remember the very first question asked of you in the *Mirror of Change? What are the three most important changes you would make in your life right now if you could?* Most likely, these three changes correspond closely to the deepest dreams you now have for your life. The truth is that you *are* capable of bringing some of the most important elements of these dreams into reality, and you are undoubtedly fully immersed in that process right now.

As you contemplate just what your deepest dreams really are, you may also wish to consider these questions:

What would you do with your time if you had only a year left to live? How would your priorities shift? What would become most compelling to you to accomplish or experience?

Create a detailed and imaginative vision of how you would spend your time if you were to live with a daily awareness of how precious it really is. Ask yourself this:

What is this vision telling you about what you truly desire and where you need to focus your energies, both in the immediate future...and in the next year of your life?

Now come up with an extraordinary vision of the future! Be as expansive as you can.

How would you like your life to look five or ten years from now, if all that you would wish for could come about? Where and with whom would you be living? What work would you be doing? How would you be spending your leisure time?

Now consider this—what are the most crucial elements of these dreams and visions?

Are there some specific goals that you can create from these elements that are within the realm of possibility for you to bring about?

What major steps can you take toward making these goals become a reality? What are some of the minor steps that you can take—this month, this week, and this very day?

I suggest you write down a vivid and detailed description of your greatest life vision. Look at it often. Continually keep it in mind as you formulate related goals, and then take the corresponding steps that will bring them into being.

Most important of all is to commit to taking at least one action every single day toward bringing your long-term goals and dreams into reality. This allows you to honor the truth of what is important to you, and to affirm the direction in which you are headed. The satisfaction of working toward our goals can also bring many more moments of contentment into our lives *right now*—even if the major rewards and greatest joy will come later. I find that even in the areas of my life where all is not yet as I would wish it to be, if I know that I am working toward the positive changes that I most want to occur, I can be much happier even in the present.

Celebrate who you are with every step you take along the pathway of realizing your greatest visions and deepest dreams!

5.

The Pathway of Creative Expression

Expanding

Your Creativity

in New & Exciting Ways

We are, ourselves, creations ...
& We, in turn, are meant to continue creativity, by being creative ourselves ...

Julia Cameron

You Are an Artist
Creating Your Life Anew in Each Moment!

Julia Cameron, in her insightful book on creativity, *The Artist's Way*, says, "We are, ourselves, creations. And we in turn are meant to continue creativity by *being* creative ourselves." For we are all artists, and along with the divine creative source, we are continual cocreators, creating our greatest works of art, ourselves—each day, each hour, each moment of our lives! As such, "We are all being called into our own greatness," affirms Jean Houston, the visionary writer, teacher, and inspiring speaker.

In these times of phenomenal change for women, men, and children everywhere, we are each being truly called. We are being called, at the deepest level of our souls, by Spirit, by the infinite, eternal, divine source of all creation and creativity, of all wisdom, of all beauty...

We are being called to create new visions for what is possible, to love at the highest level of our being, to create beauty in every way that we can. We are being called to become the most magnificent versions of ourselves possible, to become the most creative, capable, splendid, majestic selves that we can be while we walk this earth!

You, too, are being called—into *your* own greatness. I know that you hear that call, deep inside yourself, and you are acting upon it, right now, even as you read these words. This inner calling is why you are now creating new visions for what your life can be about and who you can become. It is why you *are* so clearly on the pathway to becoming the greatest possible version of yourself!

Jean Houston also says, in *A Passion for the Possible*, "We can no longer afford to live as half-light versions of ourselves. The complexity of our time requires a greater and wiser use of our capacities, a rich playing of the instrument we have been given. The world can only thrive if we can grow."

Ask yourself the following questions, and take some time to think about how you can make your life an even greater canvas for the luminous self-portrait that you are in the process of painting. Think of every way possible to grow, to expand your creative flow in new and exciting ways, to use your capacities to the greatest extent, to play the rich instrument of yourself as fully as you can!

Into what areas of your life would you most like to channel your inherent creativity—your career, family, relationships, artistic pursuits, or some combination?

Are you now engaged in work that uses your creative energies? If not, is there anything that you can do differently to make your current work situation into a more creative endeavor?

We are all
being called
into our own
greatness...

Jean Houston

Do you have a desire to change course altogether and find a new life work that can satisfy your need to use your creativity more fully? If so, what do you need to do in order to go in that direction?

What new forms of creative expression would you like to try? Can you commit to pursuing them, even for a brief time each week?

Consider your current creative pursuits. Are you ready to devote yourself more seriously to any of them, to perhaps take them to another level?

Whatever is most calling out to you in this way—pay attention to your deepest longings. As much as you can, appreciate and fully utilize your wondrous capacities to create, for they are boundless, unlimited, embedded within you, just waiting to be unleashed!

As a most marvelous way to celebrate who you are, follow that call into your own greatness. Make of your life a true work of art, and use your natural, ever-present, continually flowing creativity in as many new and expansive ways as you can!

6.

The Pathway of Spiritual Awakening

Awakening

to Your Spiritual Essence

It is this belief
in a power larger
than myself
& other than myself...
which allows me to venture
into the unknown
& even the unknowable...

Maya Angelou

You Are Forever on the Pathway of Awakening to Spirit!

True spiritual awakening is a lifelong process. It comes to each of us in different forms and at different times, and sometimes is the result of a major, life-changing event. In my own life, it was facilitated at an early age by the entrance into the world of a younger sibling. When I was nine years old, my mother gave birth to a baby boy—my brother, David, who has now grown up into a sensitive, thoughtful, and talented young man. I am glad to have him in my life, though for a time after his initial arrival, now nearly thirty years ago, his presence was a bit less welcome. He and I at first shared a room, and all too frequently, he awoke frantically crying in the night. He could not be calmed down for what seemed like hours on end, making it impossible for me to get much of a night's sleep.

Several years later, the solution seemed to be for me to move into the room which had been the family library, where massive shelves stocked with hundreds of books lined the walls. Among them were the many fresh-off-the-press books just printed by the large New York publishing company where my father spent long days as editorial director of the children's book division. These stood right alongside the huge stacks of well-worn, seemingly ancient books on every subject conceivable, accumulated by my mother's father from years long past.

It was in that room, filled to overflowing with wondrous words—where I could be no longer awakened at night by my baby brother's cries—that my real spiritual awakening began to occur instead. For my grandfather, when alive, had been an avid reader, and was also fascinated by world cultures and religions. Over the years he had collected numerous volumes that enumerated and elaborated upon the texts and ideas of the world's great religions, and these now became my reading materials of choice. Children's books began to be a thing of the past for me. Instead, night by night, I pulled from these shelves, one by one, the volumes that began my never-ending quest to understand the spiritual thinking and ideas of people the world over.

At a young age, I learned that in addition to my own, there were many other religions with rich traditions and heritages. This brought me to the realization that there simply could not be only one path to truth, for there were people everywhere who had never heard of Christianity. How could a loving God not speak to them in their own way, time, language, and thought systems? Within me arose a growing awareness that Christianity was one path to spiritual truth and understanding—yet so were Judaism, Islam, Hinduism, and Buddhism, among many others still. So my quest began, in those late-night hours of my early years, in my library-turned-bedroom, and it has never ceased, but has instead grown deeper and more expansive over time. It was, and still is, about learning to understand, honor, and appreciate the best that each unique yet universal spiritual pathway has to teach and to offer.

But as a child, and later throughout my turbulent teenage years, my quest also led me through a phase of great spiritual doubt. The world seemed so unfair, so full of pain and struggle. In my limited perception at that time, I felt that perhaps this meant that there was no higher realm, no guiding divine presence—for if there was, then why could not life be easier for us humans while we are here? *Why was all the pain, struggle, and suffering necessary?*

These deep questions—and many others, too, including what direction my own life was to take—weighed upon me that long-ago fall when I left home, at age seventeen, to go away to college. Yet once on campus, I soon settled in, and was immensely glad to finally be on my own. What a great relief it was to be away from the tremendous daily tension of life at home with my parents, who were finally coming close to the ending of their long and difficult marriage. For the first time, I was sensing what it was like to be an independent young woman. This new life phase I was entering truly seemed like a time of renewal to me, a time of exploration of new ideas and experiences.

It was one especially beautiful day, in the late fall of my freshman year, when I had a profound experience of opening to the spiritual realm in a new way, which created a permanent inner shift in my understanding of life. Between afternoon classes I decided to wander down through the large wooded area that led to a gently flowing river at the edge of the campus. The October air was crisp and invigorating, and as I walked, I felt free, light, and open. As I slowly traveled farther along the forest pathway, and approached the clearing near the riverbed, I looked up at the tall, majestic trees surrounding me—and I felt connected to them in some strange and indescribable way.

Their many elegant long branches, gracefully outstretched toward the brilliant blue sky, were covered with thousands upon thousands of golden, sunset orange, and ruby red leaves, sparkling, like exquisite jewels, in the bright, effervescent afternoon sun. Huge shimmering shafts of light seemed to beam down from above, touching the leaf-laden earth upon which I walked, perfectly illuminating my every step. I was mesmerized— the dazzling, vibrant colors danced before my eyes in every direction. I was then somehow overcome with a realization that I was not just a witness to this extraordinarily lovely scene. Instead, I was a vital part of it. I was completely immersed in the splendid colors, the luminous patterns of light, the radiating energy of life that I sensed all around me. I was alone— but for the first time in my life, I did not feel alone. I sensed the incredible presence of something far greater, more complex, and more expansive than anything that I had ever felt before.

In that moment, all the doubts that I had ever had as to whether or not there was indeed a "God" suddenly seemed to melt away. It was then that I just knew, from the center of my being, that this exquisite, all-encompassing creative energy that enveloped me was, and forever will be, *infinitely* real. And we are, each and every one of us, part of this magnificent, mysterious, universal, and eternal divine presence—which we choose to call God.

I emerged from the woods late that autumn afternoon with a forever-changed perception. I have since carried with me a deep inner knowing, a growing sense that there is a purpose to all that happens to each of us in this lifetime. This has sustained me throughout many of the most heartrending of times, ones that would have been truly unbearable otherwise. These words of Maya Angelou speak to what is now surely true for myself as well: "It is this belief in a power larger than myself, and other than myself, which allows me to venture into the unknown and even the unknowable."

This faith in a power much greater than myself is what allows me to accept that the world we live in is indeed full of mystery, for we do live in a world that is full of deep pain and suffering, tragedy, and injustice, and, much as we wish we did, we just don't have the answers to everything. Yet this world also contains an abundance of unending and unfolding beauty and immense love, as do each of our individual lives. And much of our very purpose here, as we journey through life, is to learn how to *transform* suffering—to transform it into understanding, love, and compassion—for ourselves and each other.

Spiritual awakening, I have come to believe, is about developing a great feeling of openness to spiritual truth, in whatever form it comes, from whatever source it arises…and it is indeed something to celebrate, every day…It is also about remembering that we are all spiritual beings, here in human form at this time, to live out our unique life missions. We are an integral part of the Great Mystery, the One Spirit of all that is…and there are many pathways to connecting to the divine, for it lives within each of us. The divine presence lives within you…and is all around you…

I imagine that there have been moments in your life, too, that have allowed you to experience this sense of deep connection to the divine. I believe that we all have those luminous instances, when suddenly doubts and illusions slip away, and we are momentarily immersed in that powerful feeling of connection to all that is. Yet aside from those life-changing moments of realization, there are also times when each of us can consciously bring about a deepened sense of spiritual connection.

Now consider these questions as your never-ending journey of spiritual awareness and awakening continues to unfold:

What spiritual insights have you discovered in recent years—or in times long past—that have made a difference in how you perceive and move through life?

What are the moments that shine in your memory when you have felt most spiritually attuned, awake, and alive?

When in a given day do you feel this sense of spiritual connection? Is it when reading inspirational books? Through prayer, meditation, or engaging in creative work? Through connection to nature, or other people, or participation in a spiritually oriented group?

What can you do to create more such moments that are lived in a state of spiritual connection and wakefulness each day?

Let us all find as many ways as we can to honor our innate spirituality, whether through prayer, meditation, written words, or communion with nature—whether delving deep within or in the company of our beloved ones. Let us attune ourselves ever more closely to the divine wisdom that is always present within us, awaiting our attention.

As you open yourself fully and allow the healing, calming waters of the spirit to wash over you, you will awaken once again to your true self. And perhaps more than anything, this is the pathway to truly celebrating the essence of who you are.

7.

The Pathway of Loving Kindness

Celebrating

Your Connections to those Around You

Everything & everyone is related to everything & everyone else...

E. Maria Harris

You Are Here to Celebrate Your
Loving Connections with Others!

At last we have arrived at the pathway we all need to walk upon together—that of *loving kindness*. For the purpose of every step of our journey has been to increase our awareness and understanding, that we may then come to appreciate and love ourselves, and those in our midst, to a much higher degree.

Almost all of us do consider our most joyous moments to be those when we experience a sense of loving connection with others. When we are *feeling* understood and appreciated—seeing the world through like eyes, enjoying the beauty of each other and our surroundings in a place of true harmony—many of us are at our absolute happiest. These are the times that reside in our hearts and memories forever, and are the kind of moments we are always seeking to create.

Yet for most of us, these magical, precious moments of connection and true understanding are not nearly as constant as we would wish them to be. For if loving ourselves is challenging, loving others can at times be even more so. Although on some level we are all essentially connected to one another, we don't always feel it or perceive it in the moment. Instead, conflicts, misunderstandings, and misperceptions often arise that distance us from one another, preventing us from sensing this underlying connection.

How then can we create more moments where we experience a deep, life-sustaining, loving connection to others? How can we sense—and then begin to celebrate—our connections to those around us?

Most of all, let us hold in our hearts this truth: that absolutely everyone, underneath it all, has at their core the exact same needs and wants. Every single one of us wants more than anything to be loved, honored, and appreciated—to be made to feel that we are special and important to others.

So let us give more acknowledgment to those around us whenever we can! Let us cultivate the gracious and thoughtful habit of using loving speech as often as we can, with ourselves *and* with those around us. It helps to become as aware as possible of how we are affecting others in our interactions with them. So often we don't realize that a slightly cross tone of voice or a carelessly worded comment can truly hurt those we care most about. Choose your words with greatest care and kindness, and offer as much validation and appreciation as you can to those you encounter, throughout each day.

Let us also learn to speak the words of love aloud more often. Saying the words "I love you" to those to whom it would mean a lot can be an extremely important way of honoring and celebrating our deepest connections to others. I am grateful that my daughter and I freely say these words to each other, since when I was a child, words of love were not spoken aloud in my household, ever. But I craved hearing them, and it is a truly healing gift for me to at long last have this experience of loving expression as a constant in my life. I know that I need to use these words more often with other significant people in my life, and I am still learning to practice this more often.

Let us take care to honor those closest to us in other ways also. Is there someone special in your life who would appreciate a beautifully written card or letter from you—one filled with your own heartfelt words, telling them just how much they mean to you—not just on their birthday or other special occasions, but as a lovely surprise when they are least expecting it? Is there someone who would be happy if you took them out to dinner, or sent some fresh flowers or another well-chosen gift? Or is there another kind of gesture that you can make toward someone in your life today that can brighten his or her spirit? Such things can only serve to strengthen your connection, and bring moments of beauty and joy and love into their life and your own at the same time.

What about those to whom we are connected—and sometimes wish we weren't—for they bring great difficulty to our lives?

In such situations, you may find it helpful, once again, to look at everyone around you as your potential teachers—for everyone *can* teach us something, if we look deeply for the lessons being offered. Sometimes the most unlikely teachers are presented to us, perhaps to increase our understanding, and to teach us patience, flexibility, forgiveness—or other such qualities that we may need to practice and develop.

I've had such an experience myself in the last year, in a most unexpected way. At the end of last summer, with much effort, I had finally finished rearranging my office space so that my own studio would be the room with the view of a beautiful waterfall from the windows. Comfortably settling into my new space, I was happy. It was blissfully quiet and peaceful, just what I thought I most needed to begin to immerse myself fully in the writing of this book.

Yet within days, a new tenant moved in on the floor just above me—and she turned out to be someone with a great dream of her own in the making. And her vision, now coming to life, was clashing with my own, for she was creating a dance school in the space directly above mine. The problem—and it seemed like a huge one—was that this is an old building, with little insulation and virtually no soundproofing. Soon enough, students enrolled, and classes started. The ceiling of my studio began to rumble, the walls began to shake, and the noise seemed intolerable!

I mourned my peaceful space of the past, and there were no others available, so moving within the building just wasn't an option. For a while, greatly distressed, I was sure I could never adjust. I loved the building, its location was ideal, and I did not want to move elsewhere. What was I to do? After a while, I realized that I most needed to ask myself the questions I often ask when such a difficult situation comes about: *What could be the lesson for me here? What could be the "hidden gold" in this situation for me? What was this dance teacher trying to teach me, by essentially requiring me to participate in her classes in this unusual way? What was I to become a student of right now?*

Soon came the answers. I realized more clearly than ever that the "interconnectedness of all life" is more than a spiritual or theoretical concept. Indeed, it is very much a reality—even if we sometimes wish that it were not! We are *here* to learn from each other, to accept each other's presence in our lives. And sometimes we simply must live with less than ideal circumstances, with all the grace, humor, understanding, and tolerance that we can find.

I also recognized that this situation was here to help me become ever more aware that *peace is a state of mind.* And it is one that I can choose consciously, one that can arise from within, whatever the outward circumstances. It took some time, but over the course of several months, I gradually came to shift into a new perspective. I saw that I could allow the intense vibrations that entered into my space to disturb my sense of peace. Or I could choose to hear, feel, sense, and accept them simply as spirited movements of creative self-expression, of those celebrating themselves through the joyous art of dance.

I chose then to take this second and much more positive view—and still do, for the dancers are making their presence known even as I write these words. I also appreciate the peace and quiet to a higher degree than ever before when classes are *not* in session! Since it is no longer a given, or a constant, I consider the silence a true, most welcome gift during the many hours a week when it is still present.

So let us all find ways to honor our sometimes difficult connections, and in the process, allow them to become our greatest teachers. This is often challenging—yet as Maria Harris states in *Dance of the Spirit,* "Everything and everyone is related to everything and everyone else." When we open ourselves fully to this truth, we can come to appreciate the wide web of connections we are daily immersed in and to see the special and sometimes surprising lessons in store for us.

Let's also learn to celebrate our connections to those in the wider world! By coming to a greater state of awareness of just how beautiful and radiant a spirit each one of us truly is, we can then learn to see the whole of humanity in a much greater light.

Each of us is an eternal, shining star, our individual light capable of brilliantly illuminating the night sky, gorgeous in itself…yet so much more beautiful still when we join the dazzling array of stars and suns lighting up the entire galaxy…And we are each a vital part of the endless cosmos, the infinite, magnificent, expansive whole…for it is this that we are all continually creating together…

Each one of us does contribute to the magnificent whole of humanity, yet we rarely realize just how much impact we can have on each other. The very fact that this book now exists is a testament to this, for over the last few years, many people wrote to me asking me if I was planning to put my work into book form. And their letters had a powerful influence on my decision to do so.

One early spring day in 1997 an especially heartfelt, handwritten letter from a woman in Boston came to me, urging me once more to create a book of my work. I still remember the morning I received it. I took in its gentle words of gratitude and encouragement—and wondered just how I should respond. I kept the letter in its envelope on my desk for quite some time. I read it, over and over, each time considering how my life would change were I to truly consider honoring this request.

It was several months later when I became clear that the time had come for me to indeed do so. And this decision has brought great new challenges and changes to my life each and every day since. But in the deepest moments of struggle that have arisen for me as a result of this choice, I have taken that letter out of its envelope. Its words have danced forth from that beautiful blue paper, reassuring me that yes, I *am* on the right course.

So let us write letters that express our appreciation to others whenever possible—to those we are closest to, and also to those who have inspired us from afar! Our words will inspire them in turn, and then the cycle of honor, love, and inspiration will be never-ending. Is there anyone to whom you would like to express your appreciation in this way? It may well be that your thoughts and your very words will someday affect another life in a remarkable way!

As we travel this pathway of loving kindness, let us also keep this in mind always: *Each one of us is just another soul, on a learning journey, here to heal, to learn to love, to gain wisdom, and to find our way back to the light.* We are all wounded to some extent—and we need to offer each other support and encouragement in every way that we can.

As we move through our days, we need to send as much positive, healing energy to each other as possible—and we need to receive it as well. We can do this through loving speech, kind and caring actions, and greater understanding and awareness, and by consciously sending rays of light into the hearts of those we love—*and* those we find most difficult to love.

Take a look now at the meditations that are offered on the following pages. They may be thought of as loving prayers, or as *Loving Kindness Meditations.* Their essential purpose is to allow you to open to a greater state of connection, of love and kindness toward yourself—and then toward all others with whom you share this beautiful planet.

You may wish to spend a few moments with these prayers/meditations each day. And if you like, you may make up your own versions. If you do take the time to say these or similar words—perhaps while looking into a mirror at the same time—soon enough you will begin to *feel* a greater sense of love for yourself. You will feel it also for those dearest to your heart, and by extension, for those around you in the wider world, and for the universal spirit of all that is.

This pathway of sending forth the energy of loving kindness is the clearest, most essential pathway to true inner peace, to moments of joy, and to celebrating who you are, in the deepest way possible.

Loving Kindness Meditations

Loving Kindness Meditation for Yourself

Say this loving kindness meditation/prayer for and to yourself, whenever you need to calm your mind and soothe your spirit, and as a beautiful way to start or end the day.

May I be at peace

May my heart remain open and clear...
May I always find the beauty in my own soul...
May my spirit be light and free...
May I see myself, this day and always,
through the eyes of deepest compassion...

May healing take place within me...
May I be free from anxiety, from worry and fear...
May I sense my connection to the divine within me...
May I awaken to love, and to the light...
May I walk the path of peace and insight,
throughout this day, and on into the night...

Caroline Joy Adams

Loving Kindness Meditation for Others

Now may you wish for others what you wish for yourself. Think about those you love, or those you have trouble loving, for perhaps they need your love most of all. Imagine as you speak these words that you are sending forth golden rays of light that will surround the ones you are focusing on, soothing their spirits, warming their hearts, helping them realize their own loving essence. Send your thoughts directly to them with as much love, as much kindness, as much peace and goodwill as you can. Speak these words, or a variation of your own—with reverence, with power, and with feeling—out loud or in silence, whenever you can.

May you be at peace

May your heart remain open and clear...
May you always find the beauty in your own soul...
May your spirit be light and free...
May you see yourself, this day and always,
through the eyes of deepest compassion...

May healing take place within you...
May you be free from anxiety, from worry and fear...
May you sense your connection to the divine within...
May you awaken to love and to the light
May you walk the path of peace and insight,
throughout this day, and on into the night...

Caroline Joy Adams

Conclusion

Congratulations! You have now traveled through the Seven Mirrors and the Seven Pathways. Our magical journey together is coming to a conclusion. What discoveries have you made along the way? How are you feeling about yourself now? What new visions have you come up with during this time of reflection?

I thank you from the deepest place in my heart for allowing me to be your guide through this important process of learning to honor and celebrate who you are. I hope more than anything that you will come away from this book feeling a greater sense of your own wisdom, courage, and creativity—and of your beautiful, radiant spirit.

Just imagine if all of us could live our lives in an internal space of honoring and celebration every day! How would that change the world, I wonder? My greatest wish is that future generations of girls will grow up with such inner confidence and awareness of their innate strengths and beauty that when they reach adulthood, they will already know themselves as worthy of honor and celebration at all times!

I hope that this will be true for my own daughter, for she has been and still is my greatest teacher in this regard, and in many others. Born with a look of deep wisdom in her eyes, she was actually named Elizabeth at birth. Yet she never liked the sound of that name, and fiercely resisted being called by it, even from the time she was two years old.

It was when she was seven that we took a momentous trip to the Rocky Mountains in Colorado. We slowly ascended the heights, in awe of the spectacular scenery surrounding us in every direction. At the top, she stood still for a moment, upon that majestic 14,000-foot peak, the world spread before her. Somehow, she knew who she was for the first time—and who she wanted to become. Upon the descent, she declared that she now wanted to be renamed Kristen. She has never wavered since, and I have honored her choice. I rejoice at how she is able, at such a young age, to claim such a strong, solid identity for herself. What if all of us had been encouraged to joyously proclaim who we were, from our earliest years? How would we have felt about ourselves then? And how would we now?

Yet though the past has shaped you,
it is the future that unfolds before you now…
a future that you are creating anew,
each moment of each day…

As it continues to unfold,
my deepest hope for you
is that by traveling the pathway of this book,
you will begin to take some of the
Seven Pathways to Celebrating Who You Are
to heart…
May they lead you to love, to joy,
to the manifestation of your deepest dreams…
and to many more moments of inner peace,
of calm, contentment, and beauty,
every day of your life
now and forevermore…

Acknowledgments

I give thanks first of all to my dearest daughter, Kristen, who has been my inspiration every step of the way. And to Douglas Monkton, for his ever-present enthusiasm and valuable editorial insight. And to Pat Stacey, who also offered helpful editorial suggestions along the way. And to Martha Ramsey, for her useful input at the copyediting stage. Thanks also to Jo Ann Deck of Celestial Arts, who has been a continual guiding force in the creation of this book. And to Nina Graybill, for her part in the process. And thanks to Shanna and Rinaldo Brutoco, for having originally brought my work into the lives of so many through the Red Rose Collection.

I also give thanks to all of the wonderful women and men whose presence graces my life, including those who read parts of the manuscript, or offered their friendship, love, and encouragement in other ways: Gayle White, Hila Kummins, Carol Farley, Sarah Elston, Miriam Oppenheimer, Janet Parker, Sigrid Goodman, Sal Colbert, Justina Golden, Kate Stenson, Laurel Gardner, Hillary Morgan-Cully, Jean Frances, Ethel Shaper, Bonnie and Tom Drueschel, Peter, Lee, and Emily Bliss Cudhea-Pierce, and my brother, David Knudsen—beautiful and treasured souls, each one of them! Deep thanks also to Nancy Knudsen, and Natalie, Court, and Henry Canby, for having opened their homes to Kristen's presence on such a frequent basis while I worked on the book. And thanks also to the three special boys who are such a bright presence in both my life and Kristen's—my nephew, Nicholas Canby, my "honorary" nephew, Seth Hopewell, and our good friend, Julian Buscemi.

Great thanks also to my father, Arvid Knudsen, who knew from the first that it was my destiny to become an artist and writer; my mother, Lynne Knudsen, for always believing in me; and my second mom, Jeanne Henderson, who has been a true angel in my life. Thanks also to all those who have been involved in the daily business of *Inspirations*—my sales reps, the stores that have carried the *Inspirations* product line, and all those who have purchased my work already. Thank you as well to those at Papel Giftware, Inc., who are now sharing the vision and bringing my products to a wider audience still—John Inzero and the entire product development team.

I also thank those who have generously allowed me to weave their own special words of wisdom into the tapestry of this book: Sarah Ban Breathnach, Marianne Williamson, Maya Angelou, Jean Houston, Angeles Arrien, Clarissa Pinkola Estes, Della Reese, Mary Manin Morrissey, Gail Sheehy, Noela Evans, Julia Cameron, Maria Harris, Melanie Gendron, and Thich Nhat Hanh. I thank all of you from the deepest place in my heart; the light of your presence truly shines throughout every page of this book.

Bibliography

I adore books, and always have. I live them, breathe them, could not live without them—and so it is not surprising that I feel compelled to create them as well! Books have always been my friends, my intimate companions, my teachers, and my counselors. They give me comfort and reassurance that in whatever experience I am having—especially those that are most difficult—I am not alone, for someone else has been there, too. Whatever new pathway of thought intrigues me, it, too, has already been explored by others, who are ever-present through their words to guide me along the way. For although we can easily feel alone in this world, books are one very important way that we can experience an immediate sense of connection, that we can share in the thoughts and experiences of others in a deep, lasting, and significant way.

I cannot list all of the many books that have been important to me along my own journey, but I want to share with you just fifty of my current and past favorites that are related in some way to the content of this book. And I would like to offer my deepest thanks to all of the authors whose works have contributed to my own thinking—and all of those whose books I am in the midst of right now!

Anderson, Sherry. *The Feminine Face of God.* New York: Bantam Doubleday Dell, 1992.

Arrien, Angeles. *The Four-Fold Way: Walking the Paths of the Warrior, Teacher, Healer and Visionary.* San Francisco: HarperSanFrancisco, 1993.

Bender, Sue. *Everyday Sacred.* San Francisco: HarperSanFrancisco, 1995.

Borysenko, Joan. *Meditations on the Wings of Light.* New York: Warner Books, 1992.

———. *Fire in the Soul.* New York: Warner Books, 1993.

Bridges, Carol. *The Medicine Woman Inner Guidebook.* Stamford, Connecticut: U.S. Games Systems, 1991.

Brown, Molly Young. *Lighting a Candle: Quotations on the Spiritual Life.* New York: HarperCollins, 1994.

Cameron, Julia. *The Artist's Way*. New York: Tarcher Putnam, 1992.
————. *The Vein of Gold*. New York: Tarcher Putnam, 1996.

DeSalvo, Louise. *Writing as a Way of Healing*. San Francisco: HarperSanFrancisco, 1999.

Douglas-Klotz, Neil. *Prayers of the Cosmos: Meditations on the Aramaic Words of Jesus*. San Francisco: HarperSanFrancisco, 1990.

Duerk, Judith. *Circle of Stones: Woman's Journey to Herself*. San Diego: LuraMedia, 1989.

Eisler, Riane. *The Chalice and the Blade: Our History, Our Future*. San Francisco: HarperSanFrancisco, 1988.
————. *The Partnership Way*. New York: HarperCollins, 1990.

Evans, Noela. *Meditations for the Passages and Celebrations of Life*. New York: Bell Tower, 1991.

Fox, Matthew. *Creation Spirituality*. San Francisco: HarperSanFrancisco, 1991.

Gilligan, Carol. *In a Different Voice*. Cambridge: Harvard University Press, 1982.

Harris, Maria. *Dance of the Spirit: The Seven Steps to Women's Spirituality*. New York: Bantam Books, 1989.

Houston, Jean. *A Passion for the Possible*. San Francisco: HarperSanFrancisco, 1997.

Iglehart, Hallie Austen. *Womanspirit: A Guide to Women's Wisdom*. New York: Harper & Row, 1983.

Joseph, Arthur Samuel. *Sound of the Soul: Discovering the Power of Your Voice*. Deerfield Beach, Florida: Health Communications, Inc., 1991.

Kabat-Zinn, Myla and Jon. *Everyday Blessings: The Inner Work of Mindful Parenting*. New York: Hyperion, 1997.

Levine, Stephen. *A Year to Live*. New York: Bell Tower, 1997.

Mariechild, Diane. *Open Mind: Women's Daily Inspirations for Becoming Mindful.* San Francisco: HarperSanFrancisco, 1995.

Meehan, Bridget Mary. *Affirmations from the Heart of God.* Liguori, Missouri: Liguori, 1998.

Miller, Jean Baker. *Toward a New Psychology of Women.* Boston: Beacon Press, 1976, 1986.

Moffet, Bette Clare. *Soulwork: Clearing the Mind, Opening the Heart, Replenishing the Spirit.* Berkeley, California: Wildcat Canyon Press, 1994.

Morrissey, Mary Manin. *Building Your Field of Dreams.* New York: Bantam Books, 1996.

Mother Theresa. *Everything Starts from Prayer.* Ashland, Oregon: White Cloud Press, 1998.
———. *In the Heart of the World.* Novato, California: New World Library, 1997.
———. *In My Own Words.* New York: Random House, 1996.
———. *A Simple Path.* New York: Ballantine Books, 1995.

Nhat Hanh, Thich. *Teachings on Love.* Berkeley, California: Parallax Press, 1997.
———. *Living Buddha, Living Christ.* New York: Riverhead, 1995.
———. *Peace Is Every Step.* New York: Bantam Books, 1991.
———. *Present Moment, Wonderful Moment.* Berkeley, California: Parallax Press, 1990.
———. *Touching Peace.* Berkeley, California: Parallax Press, 1992.

Nouwen, Henri J.M. *The Inner Voice of Love: A Journey Through Anguish to Freedom.* New York: Doubleday, 1998.

———. *Life of the Beloved: Spiritual Living in a Secular World.* New York: Crossroads, 1992.

Paul, Stephen C., and Gary M. Collins. *Inneractions: Visions to Bring Your Inner and Outer Worlds into Harmony.* San Francisco: HarperSanFrancisco, 1992.

Satir, Virginia. *Meditations and Inspirations.* Berkeley, California: Celestial Arts, 1985.

Surrey, Janet L., et al. *Women's Growth in Connection: Writings from the Stone Center.* New York: Guilford Press, 1991.

Taylor, Susan. *Lessons in Living.* New York: Doubleday, 1995.
—. *In the Spirit.* New York: HarperCollins, 1993.

Williamson, Marianne. *Illuminated Prayers.* New York: Simon & Schuster, 1997.
———. *Illuminata.* New York: Random House, 1994.
———. *A Woman's Worth.* New York: Ballantine Books, 1993.

Zimmerman, Bill. *A Book of Questions.* New York: Guarionex Press, Ltd., 1984.
———. *The Little Book of Joy.* Center City, Minnesota: Hazelden, 1995.

Permissions

Noela Evans quote. From *Meditations for the Passages and Celebrations of Life,* copyright © 1991. Published by Crown Publishers, Inc. Reprinted by permission of the publisher.

Excerpt from *Women Who Run With the Wolves* by Clarissa Pinkola Estes, Ph.D., copyright © 1992, 1995. All rights including but not limited to performance, translation, derivative, adaptation, musical, audio and recording, illustrative, theatrical, film, pictorial, reprint, and electronic are reserved. Used by kind permission of Dr. Estes and Ballantine Books, a division of Random House, Inc.

Mary Manin Morrissey quote. From *Building Your Field of Dreams* by Mary Manin Morrissey, copyright © 1996 by Mary Manin Morrissey. Used by permission of Bantam Books, a division of Bantam Doubleday Dell Publishers Group, Inc. Reprinted by permission of the author.

Marianne Williamson quote. From *A Woman's Worth,* copyright © 1993. Published by Ballantine Books, a division of Random House, Inc. Reprinted by permission of the author.

Sarah Ban Breathnach quote. From *Simple Abundance* by Sarah Ban Breathnach, copyright © 1995. Published by Warner Books, a Time Warner Company. Reprinted with permission of the author.

Della Reese quote. Reprinted by permission of The Putnam Publishing Group from *Angels Along the Way* by Della Reese. Copyright © 1997 by Della Reese.

Thich Nhat Hanh, from *Living Buddha, Living Christ,* copyright © 1995. Used by permission of Putnam Berkeley, a division of Penguin Putnam, Inc.

Virginia Satir quote. From *Meditations and Inspirations* by Virginia Satir. Copyright © 1985. Published by Celestial Arts. Reprinted by permission of the publisher.

Caroline Joy Adams would be delighted to hear about the
discoveries you make in your own life as you travel the pathway
of honoring and celebrating who you are. Please write to her in care of
Celestial Arts, P.O. Box 7123, Berkeley, CA 94707.